Circular Walks on the
Offa's Dyke Path
Volume 2—Welshpool to Hay-on-Wye

D1343390

The author on part of the Offa's Dyke Path near Kerry Ridgeway

Circular Walks on the
Offa's Dyke Path
Volume 2—Welshpool to Hay-on-Wye

Jeff Lomax

Mara Books

First published in July 2001 by Mara Books, 22 Crosland Terrace, Helsby, Warrington, Cheshire, WA6 9LY.

All enquiries regarding sales telephone: (01928) 723744

ISBN 1 902512 07 3

To my son David, with whom I have had many memorable walks.

Cover photograph: Offa's Dyke Path near Knighton
Back cover: Rhydspence and the River Wye

Contents

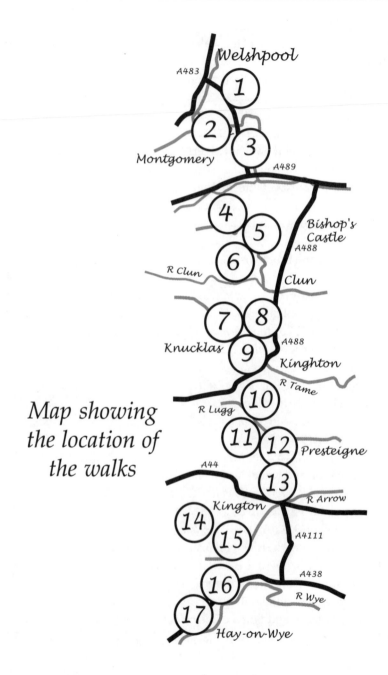

Map showing
the location of
the walks

Introduction

THIS BOOK contains 17 walks varying in distance from about 5 miles up to10½. There are shorter variations for many of the walks and, for stronger walkers, possibilities of combining up to three walks together. In total the walks cover about two thirds of the length of the Offa's Dyke Path between a point level with Welshpool to Hay-on-Wye.

The history of the Welsh Marches is very much tied up with it being a border region. The numerous valleys and ridges crossing what is now the border between England and Wales have always been routes for raids on the part of those on the Welsh side and for invasions from the English side, starting off with those of the Romans in the first century AD. The most serious incursions by the Welsh were by Llywelyn the Great and Llywelyn the Last in the 13th century and by Owain Glyndwr in the early 15th century. There are traces on many of the walks of the British who were in the area before the Romans came, but the most numerous remains are those of the Normans.

The Normans and their mottes and baileys

The Welsh Marches are effectively the product of the Normans, who were present in the area even before 1066. After the Norman Invasion King William devised a different method of rule in the border regions, to deal with the ever-present prospect of "problems" with the Welsh.

The Marcher Lords (originally the Earls of Chester, Montgomery and Hereford) were effectively kings in their own areas. They each built castles in their own "capitals" and encouraged their knights to build lesser strongholds in the areas which were delegated to them.

Many of these castles were of the "motte and bailey" type. The motte was a conical mound which could be built quickly while excavating the surrounding ditch. Initially the fortifications on top of the mound would be wooden, but the more important were often replaced by more permanent masonry. The motte was often in one corner of the larger area of the bailey (the outer courtyard), which was less strongly fortified, with a ditch and rampart (which could have a palisade on top).

These castles were very widely and thickly distributed, and can be seen on many of the walks.

Offa's Dyke

When Offa became king of Mercia (southern England) in 757 he decided to define his western boundary (and the eastern boundary of Wales) by building the dyke which bears his name.

Research has shown that Offa's Dyke was built for over half the boundary between Mercia and Wales. It is believed that Offa himself decided on the line of the dyke, and this is done very skilfully, mostly making use of west-facing slopes to give good lines of sight, even though the dyke was not generally built to be defended.

In size the dyke varies from a small bank, or even just a ledge on a steep slope, to a bank of up to 12 feet high with a ditch of similar size on the west. The variations are held to be caused by different "construction crews" as well as variations in terrain.

The finest and longest stretches of Offa's Dyke are in the area covered in this book and it features on Walks 1 to 13. After this it heads off to the east and appears only rarely as it crosses the Herefordshire Plain.

In a number of places, particularly at Knighton (the Welsh Tref-y-Clawdd [Town on the Dyke]) posts were set up for transborder trading.

The Offa's Dyke Path

The enabling legislation for the creation of national long distance walking routes was the National Parks and Access to the Countryside Act of 1999. Although the idea of a route to follow the line of Offa's Dyke was accepted in 1949, the line was approved only in 1955, and it was not until July 1971 that it was opened. There was much delay in deciding the route and then there were lengthy negotiations with landowners and much work by local authorities in creating rights of way and in ensuring that they and the existing rights of way were passable, with good stiles and waymarking.

Two events boosted the process. The first was the transfer (in 1966) of responsibility for long distance paths from the National Parks Commission to the Countryside Commission, which had more powers. The rate of progress still did not satisfy everyone, and what is now the Offa's Dyke Association was set up in 1969 initially as a ginger group to push matters forward.

The Association is still very much in business and is the prime source of information about the Path and, indeed, about the Welsh borders as a whole. They have a fine new information centre in Knighton in association with a Heritage Centre, aptly adjacent to the site of the official opening of the path. For enquiries of any sort contact:- The Offa's Dyke Association, West Street, Knigh-ton, Powys LD7 IEW.

The eventual line of the path is

almost uniformly a delight. What is not uniform, though, is the form of that delight. Connoisseurs of almost any type of British scenery will find what they are looking for at some point on the walk, the only real exception being sea cliffs (but even here there are some pretty good imitations).

Geography

This central section of the Offa's Dyke Path (ODP) crosses no less than eight rivers in addition to a number of streams and brooks. Not surprisingly there are many hills on the ODP itself and the linking paths and lanes.

Walk 1 is mainly on the eastern slopes of the Long Mountain, away from Welshpool and the River Severn.

Walk 2 touches the Severn and it and Walk 3, with which it links, both cross the River Camlad. This is the only river which rises in England and flows into Wales. However, it soon returns to England as part of the Severn.

Walk 4 crosses the ridge (which carries the historic Kerry Ridgeway) between the valleys of the Rivers Caebitra and Unk. It links with Walk 5 which straddles the Unk and a number of its tributaries. This in turn links with Walk 6, which is on the hills north of the River Clun.

Walks 7, 8 and 9 form a triad, each linking with the others, crossing and/or overlooking a beautiful winding stretch of the River Teme.

Between Knighton and Kington, Walk 10 is partly in the valley of the River Lugg, and Walks 11, 12 and 13 (which link in sequence) lie between that and the Arrow.

South of Kington, but still north of the Arrow, are Walks 14 and 15, another linked pair.

The last walks, 16, its variant 16A and 17 overlook the dramatic scenery of the Wye valley, with the slopes of the Black Mountain beyond beckoning to Volume 3.

The Reverend Francis Kilvert

Francis Kilvert is known through the diaries which he wrote, describing his life as a country clergyman. From 1865 to 1872 he was a curate at Clyro and travelled much, on foot and horseback, in the country north of the Wye in which walks 15, 16 and 17 are set.

Only three (out of 22) notebooks have survived, but reading those is an introduction to a bygone time and many interesting characters. These include Mr Kilvert himself, who had a penchant for falling in love with many of his female acquaintances. His aim of marriage was usually dashed by "poor prospects", and when he did marry, at the age of 39, he died of peritonitis a month later.

Walk descriptions

The walk descriptions start with information on how to get to the start of the walk, by car or public transport. The main route description follows, interspersed with bits of historical information and comments. The latter are in italics, so can be safely ignored.

Public transport information

All walk descriptions include information on how to get to the start by bus, and, in a few cases, by train (except Walk 8, which has no suitable buses at present). Some services are very infrequent, and there are very few services which operate on Sundays. Since the chaos immediately after the deregulation of bus services the situation has largely settled down. There are initiatives to improve rural services and there are always liable to be changes, so it is advisable to make a last check shortly before using the service. Telephone numbers of operators mentioned are as follows:

Operator	Telephone No.
Horrocks Coach Travel	01588 680354
Mid Wales Motorways	01970 828288
Owens Motors	01547 528303
Roy Browns Coaches	01982 552597
Royal Mail Postbus	0345 740740
Sargeant Brothers	01544 230481
Shropshire Link	01588 673113
Tanat Valley Coaches	01691 780212
Worthen Travel	01743 792622
Yeoman's Canyon Travel	01432 356201

If difficulties are met with (for instance if the operator changes), further information, usually including maps and timetables of services, can be obtained from local authorities, as follows:

Shropshire	0345 056785
Powys	01597 826643
Herefordshire	0345 125436

Train information can be obtained from the national enquiry number, 0345 484950.

Even for those not using cars it would be possible to do a number of these walks while staying in the same place. For instance there are links from Shrewsbury for walks 1, 2, 3, 7 and 9.

Maps

There are sketch maps with each of the walk descriptions. However it is advised that walkers also have another map covering the whole area of the walk. This will enable walkers to work out the route on a map with more information, so that it will be more obvious if the route is departed from, and ways of getting back on route can be found. The relevant maps are listed in the introductory parts of the walk description. (Note, though, that Pathfinders are being replaced by Explorers at the same scale of about 2½ inches to the mile, but covering bigger areas.) The scale of the Landranger maps is about 1¼ inches to the mile.

Precautions

Some of these walks are in quite wild, isolated countryside, so it is advisable to take precautions. Boots are certainly necessary, as there is rough ground on each of the walks. Waterproofs and extra layers of clothing are advisable and a compass could come in handy at times. In general it should not be necessary, but (for instance) if a mist comes down suddenly when on the higher hills, or if the route was lost, it could be very helpful in conjunction with a map. The only other thing to be advised (in particular if only one or two people are walking) is that someone else should know where people are walking and what time they should return, so that the emergency services can be informed if necessary.

Place names

Rather than produce a glossary of useful terms, I have tried to translate place names etc into English whenever I could. This has not proved at all easy, however. As much of the area contains few Welsh speakers, Welsh names have been corrupted so as to be unrecognisable, and reference books tend to deal with only names of major places.

The translations are in brackets [ ] after the Welsh on its first appearance in a walk. I hope that readers may find this useful, but I am sure that I will have dropped some awful clangers. For the most part I have only worked from dictionaries, which is not easy because of the way in which initial letters of Welsh words can change into other letters according to complicated rules.

It is some consolation that works of reference sometimes differ on the meaning of names! In case there is a subsequent issue of this book I should be grateful for any corrections, or translations of words or phrases I have not even attempted.

Errors & problems

I apologise in advance for any discrepancies between my instructions and what is actually found on the ground. I hope that any such problems will be caused by changes since I wrote. I am afraid that these can happen with anything - trees, hedges, fences, even rights of way can be removed or added. Again I should be grateful to be told about necessary corrections, but problems with the rights of way should be reported to the relevant local authority. These are:

Shropshire - Head of Countryside Service, The Shire Hall, Abbey Foregate, Shrewsbury SY2 6NW

Powys - Head of Countryside Access, Technical Services Dept., County Hall, Llandrindod Wells LD1 5LG

Herefordshire - PO Box 185, Hereford Education & Conference Centre, Blackfriars St., Hereford HR4 9ZF.

Acknowledgements

Firstly I should like to thank my wife Marion for her encouragement and for checking material. She has also done all the "artistic stuff" on the sketch maps.

I am particularly grateful to those who have helped by checking out the walks and subsequently giving considerable advice, namely Margaret and John Cooper, Raymond J Lloyd, Bob Nash, Jack and Carl Rogers and David Telfer.

I am also extremely grateful for information and practical assistance from the local authorities of Herefordshire ("Zog" Zveginzov), Shropshire (Terry Hughes) and Powys (Mark Chapman, Stuart Mackintosh and Carlton Parry). Without the efforts of local authority footpath officers the whole footpath network would be unusable. If only they had the resources for it all to be kept in perfect condition!

And finally ....

I hope that everyone using this book gets as much enjoyment from walking in this glorious countryside as I have done.

Jeff Lomax

Circular walks series

This book is part of a series of three volumes by Jeff Lomax which when complete will cover the entire length of the Offa's Dyke Path. Volume 1 takes in the northern section between Prestatyn and Welshpool, while volume 3 explores the southern section from Hay-on-Wye to Chepstow and should be available in 2002.

Jeff is currently working on a similar book of circular walks along the North Wales Path due for publication in 2002. The North Wales Path links Prestatyn and Bangor with extensions to the Anglesey and Lleyn coastal paths.

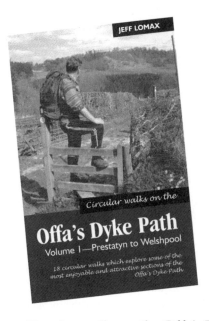

Circular walks on the Offa's Dyke Path
Volume 1—Prestatyn to Welshpool
ISBN 1 902512 01 4

Marton and Forden

A climb, mainly on lanes, onto Long Mountain, a section of the Offa's Dyke Path through the woods of the Leighton Estate and a pastoral return from Kingswood to Marton.

Distance: *9¼ miles.*

Start: *In Marton on the B4386 near the church. Grid ref. 289 026 (Landranger 126, Pathfinder 888, Explorer 216). Car parking in Marton is not easy. The Sun Inn car park is for patrons only. There is a small parking bay near houses opposite the church. It is easier to park in Forden in side roads off the B4388 near its junction with the A490. (Grid ref. 239 023) From here go north along the B4388 and turn right with a sign to Kingswood. Where the Offa's Dyke Path comes in on the left is Point 3 on the walk.*

By bus: *Worthen Travel have the 558 service between Shrewsbury and Montgomery, which runs through Marton.*

Marton is a small village but has an apparently thriving village shop (which has been associated with the same family for nearly 150 years) and the Sun Inn. The Congregational Chapel at the bottom of the village dates from 1827, the Parish Church of St Mark from 1865. There are a number of black and white houses.

In the Domesday Book Marton is referred to as Mereton [the Homestead by the Mere]. The mere (now known as Marton Pool, ½ mile east of the village) was dredged out by glaciers at the end of the Ice Age some 25,000 years ago. The pool was the reason for a community to develop here and a

Bronze Age boat which was found there is now in a museum in Shrewsbury. Much later the Roman road from Wroxeter to Montgomery probably passed through Marton.

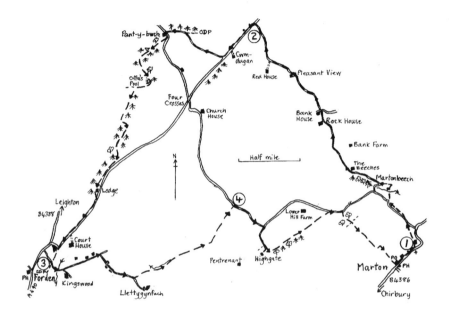

The Route

1. Start up a footpath which leads off the B4386 below a block of four houses opposite the church. Over a rise pass over two stiles and then bear right to pass the protruding corner of a barn. Bear further right to a plank bridge and stile to the left of an old oak tree with more stump than branch in the hedge ahead. From this bear right to a stile in the hedge on the right, in line with the right hand end of the top ridge of Long Mountain ahead.

The stile leads into a road which should be crossed to a gate. Go through this and turn left along the hedge on the left, passing another gnarled old oak tree. Keep along the hedge round a corner to the right (or cut across the corner) to a stile in the next hedge. Go over this and, without going out onto the road, over another stile to the right. Go through a gate just ahead and then bear diagonally left across the field towards a picturesque old wooden framed cottage.

Before the cottage go through a gate and bear right across a plank bridge over the Lowerfield Brook. Go up a track to the right of the cottage and turn left when this comes up into a field. Aim for a gate in the hedge at the top of the field but just before reaching the gate turn left over a stile. Drop down to the corner of a lane and turn right up the lane, which climbs steeply with high banks on each side. *This area is Martonbeech and the wood on the left (which seems to be all conifers and poplars) is Beech Dingle.*

After a bend to the left the chimneys of a house (The Beeches) may be seen above the bank on the right and the drive to it is soon passed. Ignore the footpath going left over open ground and a track to the right to Bank Farm as the lane continues to climb.

The view behind is developing all the time. Across the valley behind is Rorrington [Place of strong, vigorous people] Hill and the highest point of the ridge going to the right is Corndon Hill. After a bend to the right Marton Pool can be seen to the right down in the valley.

Follow the lane as it winds, now climbing less steeply and levelling off temporarily. The lane leaves Shropshire to enter Powys shortly before the buildings of Rock House Farm on the left of the lane. Go up ahead at a lane crossing where the dead end to the left passes Bank House. After another steeper section the gradient eases again before the buildings of Pleasant View Farm (which is no misnomer, even if some of the buildings are dilapidated). Continue past the drive to Red House Farm on the left.

A fine view develops to the left along the fringe of Long Mountain, beyond which is the Severn Valley. On reaching a small crest radio masts can be seen ahead, with the plantation in the Beacon Ring Hill Fort just to the left of them on the highest point of Long Mountain.

2. A T-junction marks the highest point of the walk. Turn left, with a signpost to Leighton and Forden. Pass a barn on the right and a track leading to Cwm-dugan on the left. Very soon after this, opposite a corner of wood on the left, turn right along a grassy track much used by horses. The track descends, initially between hedges, but later with more varied vegetation, including the yellow flowers of broom (in season).

At a junction of tracks the Offa's Dyke Path (ODP) joins us, having come over a stile on the right. Go left down a metalled track which descends between conifer plantations. On meeting a road, near Pant-y-bwch [Buck Hollow], turn left. Soon leave the road by going over a waymarked stile on the right and going down a path into a wood.

This is part of the Leighton Estate, which was established in its present form by a Liverpool banker, John Naylor, in the mid-19th century. An enormous amount of money was spent on the house, gardens and woodlands, possibly in a vain attempt to rival Powys Castle across the valley. The gardens were the first home of the Leyland Cypress (now infamous for its misuse in town and suburban gardens).

The path goes down at the right hand edge of the wood, with wooded slopes up to the left, and then keeps to the left of a triangular pool. From here go ahead on a forest track, which keeps level as it goes round a valley to the left. It takes a U-turn to the right round the site of Offa's Pool.

This was one of the pools which John Naylor had constructed to provide water for turbines to power farm machinery. It now holds little water, but

Marton and Marton Mere

this gives the opportunity to study the construction of the dam, with brick facing and earth backing.

After the track passes a fenced-off area for breeding game birds the ODP is signed to turn off left. It goes steeply up steps, but then levels off. *To judge from the tree stumps this section of path was cleared for the ODP. A bank which can be seen on the left is part of Offa's Dyke.*

Go ahead at an unsigned junction, but then turn left, crossing the dyke, to reach another forest track, along which the way is to the right. Soon the track comes out onto a broader one.

There is now a view down the steep slope ahead into the Severn Valley, with the buildings of Forden at the foot of the near slope. There are liable to be small planes buzzing about, from the "Montgomeryshire and Mid-Wales Airport" down in the valley.

Turn left along the wide track, which again is fairly level. Follow it as it curves round the head of a shallow valley, but when it turns to the left go ahead on a lesser track. This track descends through an area where rhododendrons are rife, with a steep slope up to the left and down to the right. After passing a stone-built lodge on the left, turn up left over a cattle grid to a road.

Turn right down the road, which is along the line of Offa's Dyke. *According to some maps it is also along the line of a Roman road, but not all experts accept this.* The road drops steadily down to the level of the valley bottom. Soon after passing the drive on the left to the large Court House Farm the road turns to the right. Continue ahead here with the ODP, passing over a stile beside a gate into a small field.

In the field bear right, along the slight ridge of Offa's Dyke, towards a hedge on the right (with houses beyond it). Go over a stile and keep to the ridge in the next field, only going down into the ditch on the right to reach the next stile. From here the ODP is an enclosed path, with a stream on the right. After a drive is joined there is a descent to a lane.

3. If a return to a car in Forden is necessary, turn right here and then left at the junction with the B4388. Otherwise turn left along the lane, ignoring the ODP, which goes right over a stile, and passing a number of new houses and bungalows. Where there is a drive to Rosehill on the right, keep left, crossing over a stream. The lane now climbs slightly to reach a fork. The farm of Kingswood is to the right, but our way is left, up a very straight section of lane.

On the climb Court House Farm is across the valley on the left and there are two modern houses (Orchard House and Coed-y-Brennin [Kingswood]) and a bungalow, The Uplands, on the left. Soon after the bungalow take a turn to the right on another straight, climbing lane, with houses scattered about on either side. *Sandywell Wood can be seen over to the left.*

The lane bears to the left to avoid the top of a small hill and then bends right to approach the farm of Lletygynfach [Little lodgings on the hill]. Leave the road actually on the bend to the right, through or over a field gate on the left.

Go along with a fence on the right until soon after passing a hut beyond the fence. Go through or over the next gate on the right and then continue, now with the fence on the left, soon with a stream beyond it. *Sandywell Wood is over to the left across the little valley.*

The path climbs up a long field and then goes through a gate into the next one, where it again climbs with the fence on the left. There are also the remains of a hedge on the left, initially (I think) of coppiced hornbeam, but later with a variety of trees. At the end of the field go ahead through a facing gate close to an angle in the fence. Bear right across the field to the far corner.

Over to the left the woods of the Leighton Estate can now be seen, with the length of Long Mountain stretching out beyond.

Go through the left of two gates close together near the corner of the field and proceed with a double wire fence on the right, with lengths of hedge occasionally in the middle. This is a long field and should only be left by a stile into the next field. Continue through the next field to reach a stile leading out onto a road.

4. Turn right along the road for about 600 yards. When the road turns to the left, turn right on an enclosed track which is waymarked as a bridleway. This soon bends round to the left. After it comes out into

an open field look for a stile in the hedge on the left and go over it.

Turn right alongside the fence to the corner of the field. Go left here, ignoring a stile on the right, with trees down the steep slope beyond the fence on the right. *This is Marton Crest.* Go through four fields (including this one), keeping to the right and going over stiles in the corner of the fields in between, descending more steeply field by field.

In the last field Lower Hill Farm is over to the left, with the Long Mountain beyond it. To the right there is a fine view across the valley of Aylesford Brook, with Rorrington Hill beyond Marton and Marton Pool.

After the four fields cross a stream on a wooden bridge, bear right with a fence on the right and, on coming out into a field, bear right to a stile near power line poles. From this bear right (keeping on the level) across the next field to another stile which leads out onto a road. Go right down the road (not the bridleway back to the right), passing new garages and houses on the left.

Soon turn right over a waymarked stile and go steeply down a field to reach a stile into a wood. The way down through the wood (mainly of oak trees) is not very obvious, but slants slightly to the left, and eventually an angle between a fence on the left and one at the bottom of the wood should be reached. Go over a stile into a field (ignoring another stile to the left) and go down the left hand side of a steep field.

Go through a gap into another field in which the slope lessens and again keep to the left. Go through a gate in the facing fence near the bottom corner and go ahead to a gate at the far end of the next field. From this continue with a fence on the right into the field corner, turn left and go to the next corner. Turn right through a gate and go up the field parallel to the hedge on the right, to reach a stile in the fence at the top, to the right of a large barn.

Go ahead past the barn to reach a stile and gate, which lead to a track down to the B4386 in Marton. The Sun Inn is opposite and turning left past the village shop will lead back to the church.

Montgomery

A walk full of history, with opportunities to explore two of Montgomery's castles. Largely flat after the initial hills.

Distance: *8¾ miles, including some exploration of Trefaldwyn Castle.*

Start: *In Broad Street, which goes westwards from the main crossroads with the B4385. Grid ref. 222 964 (Landranger 137, Pathfinder 909, Explorer 216. There is parking in Broad Street.*

By bus: *Worthen Travel have a 558 service from Shrewsbury, Monday to Saturday. Except on Saturday this gives scant time to do the walk, however.*

Montgomery owes its position to being near an ancient ford on the River Severn, once the main route from England into Mid Wales. As a consequence of this there are no less than four sites of strongholds in the area - Iron Age, Roman, Norman and Mediaeval.

The present quiet town lies below the ruins of the most recent of these and its layout is the result of mediaeval town planning. Most of the buildings are Georgian, with a few earlier remnants, and the church dates from 1225 in parts. Thanks to the efforts of the Montgomery Civic Society many of the buildings carry plaques telling of their history. A museum in Arthur Street (north from the Town Hall) gives interesting information about the town's past, much of which (as a result of its position) was violent. The town's Welsh name is Trefaldwyn [Baldwin's Town]. (The Baldwin family were Barons of Montgomery in the 12th century.)

As well as being a battleground for the Welsh and English, the town was also involved in the Civil War, with the battle of Montgomery being fought to the north of the town in 1644.

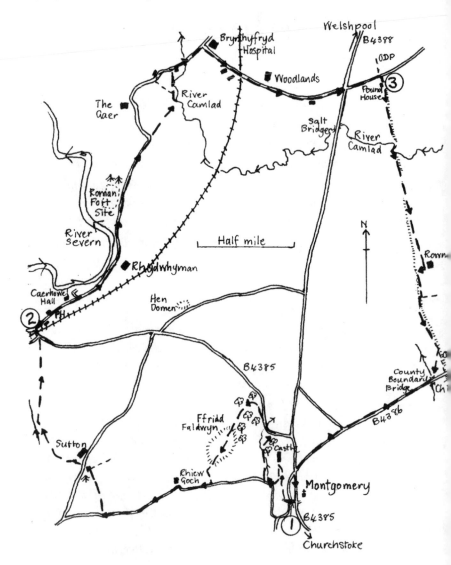

The Route

1. Start by going up Broad Street (which was once the site of the market), passing to the left of the Town Hall which was built in 1748 (and which has toilets round the back). Pass the Dragon Hotel, whose timber facing was added only in 1900, and continue up the steep tarmacked lane which is signposted to the castle. A well on the left is passed and the next houses on the left were once the Montgomeryshire County Gaol.

Looking back at this point the church of St Nicholas is prominent. Behind it, across the wide valley, is Corndon Hill, with the Stiperstones behind to the left.

Soon a kissing gate on the right leads towards the castle on a path which descends and goes through another kissing gate. A stepped path leads up to the left to the castle. There are information boards which give plenty of information about the history of the castle, which was founded by Henry III. If time permits it is well worth going round the lower level in order to get an idea of the defensive capabilities of the site, as well as going across the bridges to see the ruins.

From the far end of the castle the B4388 can be seen heading north. Offa's Dyke can be seen only as a line of trees on the far side gradually converging with it. Round to the west can be seen the ridge which is the site of the earliest fortification, the Iron Age Fort on Ffridd Faldwyn [Baldwin's Upland Pasture]. Beyond the town Lymore Park, studded with woods and pools, is best seen from the Middle Ward. (See Walk 3 for more details.)

Leave the castle by a hard-surfaced path to the left of the mound which held a dovecote (just to the right of the way the castle was entered.) Turn right in a small car park when it is reached, out onto a road. Go ahead on the road, which is climbing, passing farm buildings on the right. Just after a gate on the left of the road take a stile on the right. Go down the field, keeping about the same distance from the fence on the right to reach another stile, leading into a field which slopes down more steeply. Over to the right is a new view of the imposing castle.

The ruins of Montgomery Castle

Keep close to the decrepit fence on the right in a mixture of rose, bramble and gorse bushes, with a stream beyond it. Cross a track and, after the slope has steepened yet again, go over a stile on the right. Go down to and cross the stream and turn left in about ten yards, down through the rough wood. The path twists and turns down with a wire fence on the left, to reach a stile in a cross fence. In the meadow beyond this bear right to a stile on the left of a gate.

Turn left along the road (the B4385) beyond the stile, taking advantage of a footway on the far side, which probably owes its existence to the fact that this road led to Montgomery's (distinctly out-of-town and long-closed) railway station. After passing the end of restriction signs and curving round to the right, cross the road to a stile just before a gate. From this go past the wooden sheep pen and bear right on a slight track which rises towards the woods.

When a footpath goes straight on over a stile keep left on a track which climbs through the wood. The lower part of the wood is mainly sycamores, but higher up there are fine beeches and a few oaks. Curve round to the left, with a fence on the right, to go up the ridge of the hill. When the fence bears right keep left on the track, still on the ridge. Flattish countryside can be seen between the trees on the right.

Continue up with a grassy field on the right to the first line of fortifications of the Iron Age fort, with a clump of three beech trees and a sycamore on the right of the path. Another clump of three beeches is on the second line of defences, after which the open ground within the fort is reached.

It is thought that the site has had four sets of fortifications, the first in the third century BC. The fort originally had an interlaced timber inner rampart. The outer fortifications, with their simple gateways, came later. The style of the fort indicates that it was built by the Cornovii and fragments of neolithic pottery have been found.

There is a wonderful panorama from here, although trees block it out in some directions. To the south the War Memorial on Town Hill is prominent and to the right of that is the ridge carrying the Kerry Ridgeway. Beyond that the River Severn comes along its valley from Newtown, but is best seen round to the northwest, where this walk is heading. On a really clear day, Cader Idris may be glimpsed about 30 miles away, slightly north of west.

From the crest of the hill follow the ridge down with gorse over to the right. There are again two banks on the way out of the fort, covered in bracken, and then there is a stile, from which the path bends left towards the War Memorial to another stile, leading out onto a road. Turn right along the road which soon goes down steeply. After a double bend, right and then left, the house Rhiew Goch [Red Hill] is seen on the right.

Continue along the road, on a straight stretch which descends gradually at first and then more steeply, then bends and descends into a dip. Immediately after a bend to the right in the dip take a waymarked stile or gate on the right into a field. The waymark gives the direction to a stile in a post and wire fence. From this keep in the same direction to a field gate on the right of a small clump of trees, mainly conifers. Go through the gate here (or, probably more correctly, over two stiles to get to the same point) and go on with the trees on the left, behind another wire fence. Another stile beside a field gate leads out onto a lane, with Sutton Farm to the right.

Go across the road to a field gate and keep the fence and hedge on the right, passing a small iron gate. Turn back through a gate in the fence towards the farm and then go sharp left to go through another gate into a field. Go down the field towards buildings ahead and bear round to the right on an engineered shelf with a hill on the right. Descend past a prominent old oak tree and a power line pole to the corner of the field, with an overgrown pond on the left.

Go through a field gate and bear left towards a stream at the bottom of the field and continue with this on the left, later keeping to the right of a hedge, with the stream beyond that. At the end of the field go through the right of two gates. In the next field the route should bear right towards a railway bridge, but there is no stile on the correct line, so it is again necessary to keep to the left of the field to the next field gate. In the next field head (if at all possible) diagonally right to a field gate which leads to a road, where the way is left and then right under the railway bridge. (If the only possible way in the last field is along the fence on the left to a gate onto the road then turn right along the road and left under the railway.)

This is where Montgomery Railway Station was located, on the line from Shrewsbury to Aberystwyth and Pwllheli, which somehow managed to avoid the Beeching axe. This section of the railway was opened in 1863.

2. After going under the railway turn right onto a road towards Forden, which is followed for about 1¼ miles. Pass a garage on the right (which looks like a graveyard for Morris Minors and other cars of that vintage) and the Lion Hotel on the left. A little further on the left there is a lot of new building surrounding the mid-18th century Caerhowel [Hywel's Castle] Hall. Severn Close on the left is particularly aptly named, as the River Severn is seen below on the left just beyond it.

The next track on the right goes to Rhydwyman [Rapid Ford] Farm, named after the ford across the Severn. The site of this is just to the left and again the Montgomery Civic Society have provided an informative board. After the river bends off to the left there is a long field on the left.

At the end of this, just before a band of conifers, is the site of the Roman Fort, which originally covered half the length of the field. Looking back from here, the top of the hill to the left of Rhydwhyman Farm is the site of Montgomery's third castle, Hen Domen [The Old Heap]. This was built soon after 1066 by Roger de Montgomery (the original Montgomery in France!) who came over with William the Conqueror and was made Earl of Shrewsbury as a reward. The original construction was the standard Norman motte and bailey and it remained a stronghold (in spite of being captured by the Welsh at least once), until superseded by Henry III's castle.

Continue along the road for about a further quarter mile, until the road bends left towards a farm called, for obvious reasons, The Gaer [Camp]. Go ahead on the bend, through a gate, with what was once Brynhyfryd [Pleasant Hill] Hospital on the hill ahead. Keep the hedge on the left until the bank of the River Camlad is met.

Before going down to the river turn left over the fence, and continue with the river on the right. Stiles should be present at the next fence and, after the river has veered away to the right, to the left of a house ahead by the road. If they are not it may be necessary to get round the first fence and then head along the fence on the left to a gate onto the road near a pair of cottages. Turn right along the road (passing the cottages if the stiles were not present). Pass the house on the right and cross over the River Camlad.

Keep on up the road to a junction on the right signed to Marton. This is just before the large brick building which was once Brynhyfryd Hospital - it was for sale when I passed so could be anything by the time this is read. This building was founded in 1792 as the Montgomery and Pool Union Workhouse and covered a wide area, including Chirbury.) Turn right and go up the road, passing two small rows of houses on the right.

Immediately after the houses the road passes over a railway in a cutting and then climbs to Woodlands Farm, which is on the left. The road dips and rises again, heading towards Corndon Hill and bends right and left, with the War Memorial on Town Hill again prominent beyond Montgomery to the right. After passing a rather unexpected electricity substation on the right carry on along the road, cross the B4388 and go on for another 300 yards, until an Offa's Dyke Path (ODP) sign is seen, indicating the need to turn right on a track.

3. Go along the track, with Pound House on the right, beyond which the track has hedges on both sides, that on the left being on Offa's Dyke itself. Shortly before a gate across the path, go right over a stile and then left to have the Dyke and hedge on the left. At the end of the field go right to cross the new (1985) bridge over the Camlad to enter Shropshire. Turn left, with the river on the left until it goes further away.

Continue with the hedge and Dyke on the left, crossing a small ditch and bank in mid field. At the end of the field go ahead with a hedge on the left and a fence on the right. When there are two gates ahead go through the one on the left onto an enclosed path. Pass a deserted house on the right and ignore a stile on the left. Another abandoned building on the right has a roof of corrugated iron. Offa's Dyke is clearly to the right now, and after going through a gate we go further from it as we keep on the left of the field up to Rownal Farm.

The ODP keeps to the right of the farm, leaving the field by a stile further on than the farm gate. Turn right on the track from the farm for about 50 yards and then turn left through a bridle gate. Go through the field with the fine bank of the Dyke on the right.

I saw a hare on the bank here, sniffing and pawing the air before deciding it was safe to go onto the field. Only when he did so did he realise I was there and hare (of course) across the field.

At the end of the field (where Walk 3 joins in from the left) go over a stile on the right and turn left, now with the Dyke on the left. *The Dyke is in splendid shape here, with a definite ditch between the path and the bank. Montgomery can be seen to the right now.* Go through a gap into the next field (with Rownal Covert on the left) and continue with the Dyke on the left, soon crowned with large oak trees. Having gone through the gate at the end of the field it should be possible to go diagonally across the field to the right to a stile in the corner of the field (leaving the ODP). (Otherwise continue along the edge of the field to leave it by a gate.)

In either case turn right along the road (the B4386 from Montgomery to Chirbury), going across the insignificant, accurately but unimaginatively named, County Boundary Bridge in the dip. The road is followed back to Montgomery and requires care as it is undulating and has no footway until after a crossroads, after which the road has buildings on both sides. *A milestone indicates that it is 21 miles to Shrewsbury.* Go up the hill past the Bricklayers Arms to a crossroads with the B4388. Either the road ahead or that to the left will get back to Broad Street.

The left turn passes (on the left) various churches, some converted to homes and the old Charity School. After a milestone giving 169 miles to London turn right into Broad Street.

Chirbury

Mostly through level farmland with hills only in the distance. A nice stretch by the River Camlad.

Distance: *8 miles, but there are alternative ways back to Chirbury making it as little as 6 miles.*

Start: *At the shop and PO on the A490 heading out to the south. Grid ref. 261 984 (Landranger 137, Pathfinder 909, Explorer 216). Park on the road near the shop.*

By bus: *Worthen Travel run the 558 service between Montgomery and Shrewsbury.*

Chirbury (Church and Fort) which may be as old as Offa's Dyke itself, may have been built to guard the Dyke, and was certainly fortified, being referred to in a document of 913 AD. (A mound, which is all that remains of the fortification, can be seen down the road to Montgomery, on the right of the road just beyond the first dip.)

There is no record of the church of 913, but the present church is a fine building. Once part of an Augustinian Priory, it survived the dissolution of the monasteries by being the parish's part of the buildings. The immediate impression of the large church is one of imminent collapse, as the pillars between the nave and the side aisles very obviously lean outwards. This may have been due to a previous roof. The present one was put on in the 16th century. It is heavily braced and the outside walls are buttressed, which has prevented further spreading.

As a result of robbery the church is not normally open, but access can be arranged. It is well worth a visit. Many of the other buildings are old, notably the school, which dates from the 17th century and the adjacent half timbered school house. The Herbert Arms is near the church.

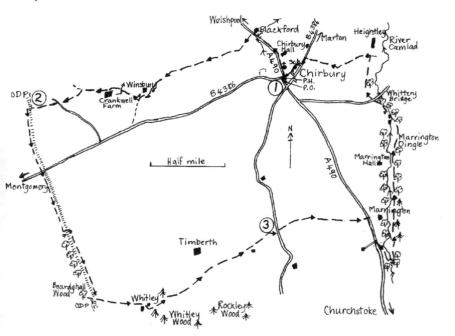

The Route

1. Turn right coming out of the Post Office and then right again to pass in front of the Herbert Arms. Turn left before the church to head out on the busy A490 (which has only a discontinuous verge) towards Welshpool, soon passing Chirbury Hall farm. The road swings round to the left and goes down to a narrow bridge. Pass the redbrick fronted buildings of Blackford on the right and cross to a stile beside the next gate on the left. Follow the track across the open field.

Looking to the left you can see that there is a range of hills behind Chirbury. More or less behind Chirbury from this angle is Corndon Hill, and Roundton and Todleth Hill are further round to the right.

At the end of the field go through the left of two facing gateways and go down the large field on a grassy track with a hedge on the right. *The farm ahead is Winsbury and the hill behind it to the left is*

St Michael's church, Chirbury

Town Hill, above Montgomery, with Ffridd Faldwyn [Baldwin's Upland Pasture] (traversed on Walk 2) to its right.

Go through the gap into the next field and continue with a neatly laid hedge on the right. From the gate and stile at the end of the field head away from the hedge on the right to a stile in a post and wire fence in line with the farm. From the stile head towards a large metal barn to reach a metal bridle gate in the far corner of the field. Go through the gate onto a track which has cottages on the left and then bears right, with other buildings on the left before joining the main lane from the farm.

Go out through the white-painted gates, pass a house on the right (Little Winsbury) and soon turn right to cross two small fields by means of obvious stiles. *The humps and bumps in these fields look as though they should have some historic significance, but the Ordnance*

Survey map reveals nothing. In the next field the way is down towards a large oak tree in the far hedge. Go over the stile and bridge on the left of the tree and go towards Crankwell Farm, with a fence on the right.

Keep to the right of all the farm buildings and go down on the track until a waymark indicates a path to the right. Ignore this, keeping on the track down to a gate in a hedgeline. From the gate bear right into the far right corner of the field, converging with a line of power line poles, and leave the field by a field gate. Cross a track and go through another field gate. In the next field go past a large oak tree in midfield and go through a gap in the ridge of Offa's Dyke to a gate and stile. *At this point you are joining the Offa's Dyke Path (ODP) and also, for a short distance, Walk 2.*

2. Once over the stile (or through the gate) turn left, with the substantial ridge and ditch of the Dyke on the left, and Montgomery to the right, with its church prominent. Go through a gap into the next field, with the remains of Rownal Covert across the Dyke on the left, and continue, now with fine oaks on the Dyke. *After the gate into the next field Walks 2 and 3 diverge, Walk 2 bearing off to the right.* This walk continues ahead (now with a hedge on the Dyke) to a gate leading onto the B4386 Chirbury to Montgomery road.

Cross the road to continue alongside the Dyke, the ditch of which is now more prominent. The Dyke climbs, with oaks being replaced by gorse as its crowning glory. Go through gates into the next field, which is a short one, and either through a gate or over a stile into the next, with a hedge on the Dyke again. Go over the crest of the hill. *To the right ahead can be seen the parkland of Lymore Park. This surrounded the fine half-timbered mansion of Lymore Hall from 1675 until the hall was, sadly, demolished in the 1930s.*

At the end of the field go over a stile, crossing the Dyke, and continue with a wood on the right behind a hedge, mostly of hawthorn, on top of the Dyke. Cross a ditch part way along the field and two stiles in quick succession at the end of it, followed by a little rough woodland before regaining the "normal" position with the Dyke on the right. We are now past the wood on the right, but there is soon another one, Boardyhall Wood. At the end of the field the ODP goes right, but we turn left along a tarmacked farm track with a hedge on the right. The track heads towards Whitley [White wood or clearing] Farm, which is seen ahead, almost surrounded by trees. A cattle grid is passed over between two fields. Turn right on the tarmac at the farm and almost immediately bear left on a rougher track to a gate. Another gate soon leads into a patch of woodland.

Very soon bear left with a blue bridleway waymark into a field. Keep to the left of the field with a fence on the left and a wood behind that. *The main part of Whitley Wood and Rockley Wood are over to the right*. At the end of the wood on the left keep ahead to another gate and then fork right with the yellow footpath waymark under or over debarbed wire (which is common in this area). Take the line across the next field from the waymark to reach a stile in a hedge about half way between a double-trunked oak tree and the next large tree to the right. From the stile cut over to the hedge on the right and continue beside this through the next field. *Timberth farm is over to the left*.

From the stile at the end of the field go ahead, keeping about the same distance from the hedge on the left, until the brick Timberth Cottage (probably much extended) comes into sight ahead. Go through a gate to the left of the cottage and then over a stile to join the track from the cottage. Follow the hard-surfaced track, which has a passing-place midway, to a road.

3. Turn left along the road. If the shortest way back to Chirbury is required continue along the road. Otherwise turn right over a stile in about 40 yards and follow the direction on the waymark across the field to pass through a hedgerow near the smaller of two oak trees. Continue down the field in the same direction to a stile which leads to a footbridge over a stream. Go up the next field with a hedge and fence on the right and a house beyond the fence.

From the stile at the top of the field bear slightly right and downhill to the next stile at the right of a single tree. Bear rather more to the right in the next field towards the right end of the Corndon Hill ridge. This leads to a footbridge and stile midway between two oak trees. From this head to another stile in line with the left end of farm buildings ahead. This leads out onto the A490.

Turning left would lead back to Chirbury, but to continue the walk go right, again with care along the busy road. Pass the drive to the farm at Marrington on the left and then that to Marrington Cottages on the right. Soon after this cross the road to a gate labelled "Private woods" with a stile beside it. Go over the stile and turn right down a track which bears left over a bridge which is functional rather than beautiful.

The bridge passes over the River Camlad, which is also seen on Walks 1 and 2. The river rises on the far side of Corndon Hill, coming round the south of it and Todleth Hill before heading north to meet the Severn between Montgomery and Welshpool. The river has cut down through a number of different geological strata to create the narrow valley of Morrington Dingle.

After going over the bridge keep round to the left for the pleasant walk through the dingle, with the Camlad on the left for most of the time. Go through a facing gate on a good track and when this splits go ahead through a gate or over a stile into a riverside meadow.

There are likely to be lots of pheasants about, as birds for shooting (rather than coppiced trees) now seem to be the main "crop" in the woods. There seems to be an element of irony in the notice which refers to the area as being a "game and wildlife conservation area".

Ignore all turnings to the right and keep fairly close to the river. *There are a sprinkling of ornamental trees about when in the vicinity of Marrington Hall, which is at the top of the opposite bank. Parts of the hall date from 1595, but the ownership is documented from the 13th century. It was in the ownership of Lords Craven in the 17th and 18th centuries. Beside the river is an occupied building which was presumably a mill.*

When the track next forks the left hand one goes into a new plantation, so take the right fork and climb for a short distance into the woods. The track is then fairly level for a while until it slants down to cross the Camlad near Walk Mill, which appears to have been converted into dwellings. Continue along the lane past the partly half-timbered Carvers Cottage, with an incongruous new conservatory. In a field on the left are three shacks, two of wood, one of brick.

When a road is reached the road to the left (as always) leads to Chirbury. To continue on the last stretch go over a stile opposite and climb the field through gorse to the edge of a wood. *Look back to see the nicely arched bridge over the Camlad and the curve of the wooded Marrington Dingle, with Whittery Wood on the left.*

Turn right along the fence to a gate which leads out into a field. *The pattern of the rights of way ahead indicates that this must have been several fields at one time.* Head towards the farmhouse of Heightley, initially along the fence on the right, until you are under power lines, with a stile over to the right. Turn left here to a stile beside a field gate.

From the stile head diagonally left up the field to reach a stile in the top hedge beyond a wooden field gate, an oak tree and a metal field gate. *From the stile there is a good view of Chirbury, with the church standing proudly over it.* Go directly down the next field to a field corner and a stile. Once over this go along a level field with a hedge and fence on the left to reach a road (the B4386 to Marton), with the house Monksfield to the right.

Turn left along the road which (with the help of a right turn at the crossroads) leads back to the start of the walk. An interesting short diversion is to turn right along a one-way road signposted to the school. The road is tightly enclosed and turns left to the school playground where the schoolhouse and school are on the right. Go straight through the playground to a metal gate which leads into the churchyard. Continue through this to pass in front of the Herbert Arms and turn left to the Post Office.

Pentreheyling

A fine walk through Mellington Woods and over the Kerry Ridgeway to the valley of the River Unk. The views and the earthworks of Offa's Dyke are fine.

Distance: *9 miles, which could be split into two loops of 7 miles (north) and 3¼ miles (south) using the Kerry Ridgeway road as a link.*

Start: *At the road junction in Pentreheyling, which is on the A489 road about 2½ miles SSE of Montgomery. Grid ref. 243 929, (Landranger 137, Pathfinder 909, Explorer 216). There is some room for parking on the verge near the junction. Otherwise the most suitable place is probably on the verge of the road northeast from the Kerry Ridgeway at 236 896.*

By bus: *There is a Minsterley Motors service on Tuesdays from Pontesbury and Bishop's Castle, but this gives time only for the northern loop, if that. This also applies to the Monday to Saturday Arriva Cymru service from Newtown. There are also occasional 778 buses run by Mid Wales Motorways from Newtown on Saturdays and Tuesdays.*

There is very little at Pentreheyling [Heylin's village] with the rather surprising exception of a cafe (with parking space) on the main road westwards towards Sarn and Kerry. Pentreheyling House dates from the 17th century and traces of a Roman fort and marching camps have been found in the area.

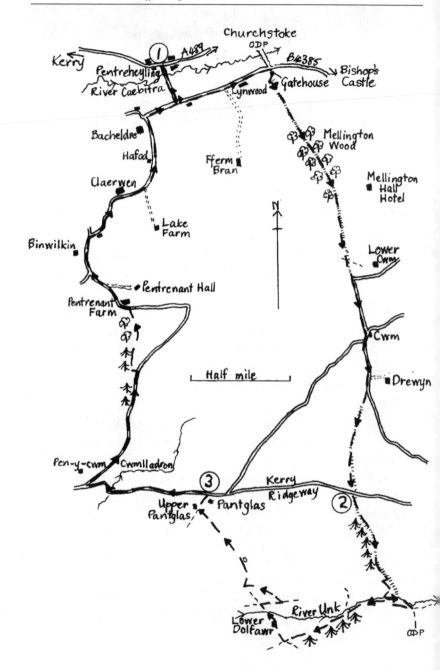

The Route

1. Start on the road towards Bacheldre and Mill, heading south from the A489. Cross over the River Caebitra (which rises in Clun Forest and joins the Camlad at Churchstoke), leaving a loop of Shropshire to enter Powys. *On the right the mill is now the centre of a caravan park.* Continue along the road to a T-junction and then turn left. Pass a bungalow on the right of the lane.

Continue along the lane, passing a road on the right (going to Fferm Bran [Crow Farm]) and Lynwood Farm (both on the right), to a corner of the B4385 road. The Offa's Dyke Path (ODP) is joined here by turning right through the wrought iron gates under an archway. *This was built as the main entrance to Mellington Hall, but the road to that now starts a little to the east. The gatehouse is reputed to be much more pleasant than the hall of 1876.*

Before reaching the present drive turn right down into woodland to a stile with a pleasant stream on the right. From the stile bear left as indicated along the bank of Offa's Dyke, with a ditch down to the right. After a short stretch through the wood a stile leads out into an open field, where the ODP goes along the right-hand side, with the Dyke to the right.

The path goes over a facing stile into Mellington Wood some distance before the end of the field. The path is soon back on top of the Dyke, where care is needed because of holes. The next stile is level with the edge of the field to the left and then there is a plantation of poplars to the left.

After this there is open ground to the left again as the path on the Dyke rises gently, accompanied by a line of poplars, but with sycamores and other acers about.

There are steps on each side of a track which cuts brutally through the dyke, with Mellington Hall to the left. Further on there are chalets and a caravan park, all in the grounds of Mellington Hall. A gateway in a stretch of wall to the right probably led to paths through the grounds in the heyday of the hall. The Dyke continues in a finger of wood and is back into farmland after another stile, where the easier walking is in the left of the Dyke.

The author on part of Offa's Dyke near Kerry Ridgeway

To the left is the farm of *Lower Cwm (Valley)*. The top of the Dyke must be regained for the last few yards to a stile which leads to steps down to a road. Go ahead along the road with a sign to The Cwm and Pantglas [Green Valley]. The road goes down initially—unfortunately, in view of the climbing which lies ahead.

At Cwm the Dyke Gallery is on the left and to the right is a pleasant group of black and white houses. In the field in front of these I have seen matching speckled sheep called Jacob's Sheep (for reasons explained in Genesis Chapter 30).

Ignore roads to the left and right and start the serious climbing up the road to Mainstone. Pass the drive to Drewin Farm (which is on the left) and in about 150 yards, just after a bend to the left, take a stile on the right. The ODP goes steeply uphill on top of the bank of the Dyke, which is soon a massive construction with a deep ditch down on the right.

There are a lot of trees around the Dyke which at times mask the glorious views which are all around, particularly back into the plain, with Mellington Hall more or less down the line of the Dyke, surrounded by trees. Beyond it is Churchstoke, with Todleth and Roundton Hill to the right of it. Heath Mynd is still further to the right, with Stiperstones in the distance behind it. To the left of the valley is Montgomery (see Walk 2), with Town Hill to the left of it and Ffridd Faldwyn [Baldwin's Upland Pasture] behind it.

The path is clear, and easy to walk except where it has been excavated, probably by badgers. Cross a track, which leads to an old quarry on the right. The gradient starts to ease off, still with trees (notably oaks) around and the height of the Dyke also lessens. After a stile the path is on the right of the Dyke, with a line of coppiced trees in between. At the next gate and stile the remote buildings of Nyth Bran [Crows Nest] can be seen on the left. The path continues as a cart track in the ditch of the Dyke to a gate and a stile to the right which lead onto a road.

This road is the Kerry Ridgeway and is on the line of an ancient track, dating from the Bronze Age. To cut the walk down to just the northern loop turn right along the road to point 3 at Pantglas (Green Valley).

2. To continue cross the road to a stile and go through gorse to another stile, beyond which to the right is a small pool. *When I first passed this, the party I was with were startled by a heron noisily taking off from the pool.* The path switches over to the left side of the Dyke, still climbing slightly. Soon there is an evergreen wood on the right. Beyond the next stile the path starts to descend and bends round to the right.

Ahead now is Edenhope Hill, which Walk 5 goes over , with the valley of the River Unk lying between. The Dyke is now minimal, but the ground slopes steeply down from it to the right.

Look out for a stile on the right from which there is a clear path down through the wood, at first on the Dyke, with hazel trees and some fine oaks about, and then going down more steeply through coppiced hazels. *(It was, presumably, because of the hazels that this is **Nut** Wood.)* The path leads onto a track which goes down more gently to the left to where a waymark indicates the way to the right across a bridge over the River Unk.

My first visit here was in a very hot summer, when there was not a drop of water in the river.

From the bridge bear left to reach a gate and stile. Walk 5 comes from the left along the valley and goes over the stile to take up the baton of following the ODP. There is a good view down the Unk valley from here, with Nut Wood on the left.

About ten yards before the stile, at a clump of small trees the route now turns sharply back to the right and takes a path which curves round to the left. Keep on a shelf with the hillside going up to the left, rather than following sheep tracks down to the river.

The upper Unk valley opens up ahead when the river is close by on the right. The track has the feel of a drove road along which sheep and cattle were driven to feed the hordes in London and other English cities.

At a field gate go right on a track towards the river but, before the bridge, turn back left up a track. Soon there is a gloomy coniferous wood immediately on the left. After a gate the path is effectively in the wood with a fence on the right, with the trees on the right mostly deciduous. *Down in the valley to the right the Unk follows a meandering course.*

The track climbs gently and a forestry track joins it from the left. When a second track comes in from the left turn right to go through a gate on the right and (if possible) go down between lines of trees and pass through two gates into the farmyard at Lower Dolfawr [Great Meadow]. Go to the right of the house and then pass to the right of stables. Follow the concrete track, which then winds down to the left to cross the river.

Turn right at a junction of tracks and keep on the track until it reaches a gate. Turn back left here onto a path which goes up across the slope through gorse and heather. *The valley of the Unk can be seen curving round to the left.* In the upper stages the path is on a broad shelf, with a double wire fence to the right. When there is a gate on the right, near an angle in the fence, go through it.

Go up the field in a groove, with a fence and a line of hawthorns on the left. At the end of the field go through or over the facing gate and then bear slightly left, with a fence on the left.

There is soon a pool (or perhaps, in view of its upland situation, a tarn) on the right and, beyond it, a windbreak of conifers. The mound beyond that looks distinctly manmade, but the OS map gives no information.

On the top of the hill pass a triangle of young conifers. Although there is supposed to be a right of way in the field on the left it is practicable only to continue along the track, with the fence on the left, going through two gates across the track. After the second gate the fence is on the right. After going through another gate go right down a tarmac lane, passing Upper Pantglas [Green Valley] on the left and Pantglas on the right. Soon the Kerry Ridgeway is met again, and the way is left along it.

3. As the road climbs there is a new pond to be seen down on the right and there are soon fine views to the right over the plain. *The steep gorge on the right is Cwmlladron [Valley of robbers], and it is not difficult to imagine footpads disappearing into it after robbing travellers along the Ridgeway.* The road drops down, bends left to cross the Cwmlladron stream and bears right as it climbs again.

Pass an old railway truck and, just before a cattle grid on the Ridgeway, turn back right down a side road. The farm of Pen-y-cwm [Head of the Valley] is over to the left. The road drops fairly steadily and after a couple of bends there is a larch plantation on the left. When there are gates on each side of the road, just before a bend to the right, go through the gate on the left. Bear right, initially down a shallow valley, and then on the right side of it.

At the bottom of the hill Pentrenant [Brook Village] Hall is obvious, swimming pool and all, with Lake Farm beyond and to the right. In the middle distance, beyond both of them, is Pentreheyling, about 1½ miles away. Churchstoke may be made out further to the right, with Todleth Hill behind it. The land looks very fertile and there are many farms.

Follow the path down a groove with a wood on the left and go through a gate. Keep close to the fence on the left, behind which is the wood. Keep down in this way through three fields to reach a road.

There is an interesting structure on top of one of the buildings of Pentrenant Farm opposite, which seems to be an old metal weathervane and bell with the addition of TV aerials. The farm itself dates from the mid l7th century, about 200 years earlier than the hall behind it.

Turn left along the road, noting the interesting farmhouse on the right. On the right the entrance to the farm is first passed, and then the entrance to Pentrenant Hall itself, which has elegant gateposts, even if they are not in use. A stream runs on the right of the road to a junction by a telephone box. Keep on ahead here now with the stream behind the hedge on the left. Binwilkin Farm is over to the left.

At a junction by a postbox turn right. There is soon a red brick building on the right and, after a few bends, Claerwen [Bright water] is on the left. The next landmarks are a track from Lake Farm, which is on the right, and a detached house, Hafod [Summer Dwelling], on the left. The next large farm on the left is Bacheldre [Home of small nook], which has l7th century buildings, and soon after this there is a right turn at a T-junction. A left turn at the next junction leads back to Pentreheyling.

Colebatch

This is a strenuous walk with plenty of fine pastoral scenery and a dramatic, switchback section of Offa's Dyke.

Distance: *10½ miles but the walk can be split into 2 or 3 by using the roads which cross the route.*

Start: *At the crossroads on the A488, about 11 miles north of Knighton. Grid ref. 318 870 (Landranger 137, Pathfinder 930, Explorer 216). Parking is a problem. It may be possible to park off the main road a little to the north. Alternatively there are spots on the road to Cefn Einion between 1½ and 2 miles along. Best is the verge near the church at Churchtown (point 3). Grid ref. about 264 873.*

By bus: *There is a Horrocks Coach Travel 766 bus which leaves Bishop's Castle at 8.10 (calling also at Cefn Einion and Mainstone), returning at 15.34, which enables the walk to be done in sections. There are also buses (numbered 742, 743 and 745) which start at Bishop's Castle (Tuesday to Saturday) or Clun (Monday to Friday), outward by Royal Mail Postbus, return by Shropshire Link.*

Colebatch [Stream valley of man named Cola] is no more than a hamlet on the road between Bishop's Castle and Clun, but had a Norman castle, probably associated with a Lefroy de Colebech, who was around in 1176. There are black and white houses along a lane leading east off the road to Bishop's Castle near the crossroads, one of them looking like an illustration in a children's book of the House that Jack Built, or even the Crooked Man's house. Apart from a telephone box to the north there are no facilities.

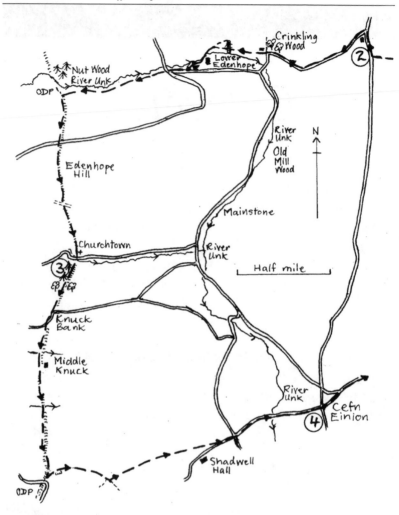

The Route

1. Start along the side road towards Cefn Einion [Anvil Ridge], with farm buildings on both sides of the road. After about ¼ mile ignore a stile in the right hand hedge, but in about 20 yards turn right along a track, with field gates to either side. Soon cross over a stream on a concrete bridge and go over a stile beside a gate ahead. Turn left into a flat meadow and go through this, keeping near the slope on the right (where, initially, there is an old quarry, now with trees growing

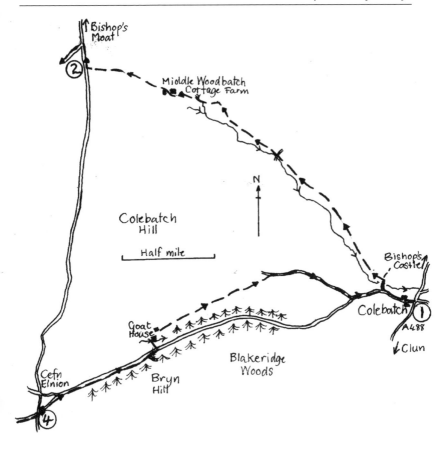

in it). Over to the left the stream is also tree-girt and there are specimen trees scattered up the slope, giving a parkland feel.

A gate and stile in a crossing fence lead into the next field, at the end of which is a stile beside the stream. The path keeps close to the fence on the left in the next field, and a waymark indicates that we are currently on the Shropshire Way. The next gate and stile are a little way from the field corner on the left and the stream is further away as the path goes to another stile in the far left corner, under a large oak tree. In the next field the stream is in the field, and the path passes between it and a small dingle and then keeps roughly parallel to the stream to the end of the field, where the stream bears left.

The path passes through gates either side of a track, then keeps to the left of a short field to another gate. In the next field head for a gate 30 or 40 yards up from the left hand corner and keep the same distance from the stream in the following field, crossing a shallow valley mid-field.

The right of way should go through one or two gates in the corner of the field up to the right and turn left along a track descending the next field. If this is not possible go through a gate about 50 yards from the top of the field and go ahead towards an ash tree in mid-field, joining the track from the top corner of the last field. In either case follow the track down to cross a stream and then climb, with a line of trees on the left, to Middle Woodbatch Cottage Farm.

Keep left of the main farm buildings and then turn right through a gate, climbing to pass to the right of a stone farmhouse with a brick extension on the left. Continue to climb on the fenced track, with a bend to the left half way towards the T-junction with the Cefn Einion to Bishop's Moat road. *Looking to the left towards the end of the track, the rounded hill is Colebatch Hill, with Henley Wood on its left end. Ahead at the junction (slightly to the left) is Edenhope Hill, over which the Offa's Dyke Path (ODP) runs.*

2. Turn right along the road for about 250 yards and then turn left immediately after a pair of cottages on the left. Go down the road, which is signed to Mainstone [Stonestone!], for just over half a mile. *On the first stretch the valley of the River Unk is ahead, with woods on each side, the one on the left being Old Mill Wood, on the lower slopes of Reith Top.* After two slight bends to the right a bridge over the river can be seen down to the left. Crinkling Wood is on the right where the road bends sharply left to go over the bridge.

Leave the road at the bend, going ahead through the left of two gates. Keep a fence on the right at first and then follow a faint track to the right. Once over the crest of the hill the right of way should pass through the band of conifers ahead about 30 yards up from the stream and then bear slightly right to meet a track coming from the right. Unless this seems likely it is safer to aim into the top corner of the field, where the band of thick, windbreaking conifers coming up from the stream to the left meets another band of conifers at right angles. Go left through the gate and down the track towards the right end of the conglomeration of buildings at Lower Edenhope Farm, joining the right of way about half way along. Ford the River Unk (it is seldom more than a few inches deep) and keep to the right of the main farm buildings. Turn right to pass to the left of the farmhouse and continue on up to a road.

Go ahead on the road and continue along to a slanting T-junction. Go across the road and through a gate. Follow a slight track which gradually converges with the fence on the right and go through a gate in the corner of the field. In the next long field keep fairly close to the winding river on the right to reach another gate in the next crossing fence, just to the left of a clump of trees. The next field is similar, with Nut Wood now across the river; head towards a plantation which appears above the ridge of Edenhope Hill ahead. Eventually there is a line of stunted trees on the right of the path.

Just beyond a gate on the left is a stile with an Offa's Dyke Path acorn waymark. Go over the stile to join the ODP and go up the field with a fence on the left. *Beyond the fence is Offa's Dyke itself, which, for this stretch at least, is being protected from the ravages of many pairs of feet. This is fine from the archaeologist's point of view, but the soft grass and soil of the field do not make easy walking when wet, and will soon be seriously eroded.* As the gradient increases the ODP bears right towards a waymark, with a wood over to the left, beyond the Dyke. *Behind are the lines of (mostly) conifers in Nut Wood, with the line of the Dyke (and Walk 4) showing up slanting over to the left as a line of deciduous trees.*

Once the wood on the left is passed the gradient gradually eases off to a stile on each side of a crossing road, after which a gentle ascent leads to the top of Edenhope Hill, with the path now back on top of the Dyke. From the stile on the very top there are fine views. *To the west (right from this route) is the complicated terrain of the Clun Forest area and to the east the Long Mynd may be seen on a clear day. Ahead is more hilly country to be negotiated, but first there is a very steep descent into the Churchtown Valley.*

From the top of Edenhope Hill the ODP descends along the top of the Dyke. The first stile on the descent is where a farm track crosses, and the path then returns to the top of the Dyke. The descent is very steep on the next section and it is good to have a solid surface under one's feet. *Ahead, across the valley, the ODP can be seen climbing up through Churchtown Wood.* After another stile the slope eases off a little, and the next stile leads out onto a road at Churchtown.

"Town" seems inaccurate, as there are very few dwellings about, but St John the Baptist's Church, the parish church of Mainstone (which is a mile away), is close by to the left. The church was rebuilt in 1887, but some old features remain, notably the unusual panelling at the top of the walls and the Elizabethan woodwork of the roof. The font is believed to be 12th century, and a large stone near the pulpit (perhaps the original "Maenstone") is reputed to be for weighing grain for selling across the border formed by the Dyke. It is said that the siting of the church is due to the fact that attempts to build in the village were thwarted by the stone repeatedly being mysteriously moved to the present site.

If time is pressing or energy waning it is possible to save about 1¼ hilly miles by turning left along the road. Turn right at a T-junction

Churchtown

in about half a mile, keep on ahead at the next junction and climb to a crossroads. Going ahead here will rejoin the "official" route at the next junction; turning right will lead to the crossroads in Cefn Einion (Point 4).

3. To continue the walk cross over the road from the way down from Edenhope Hill and go over a stile and a footbridge across a stream, then another stile indicating that we are now on Wild Edrik's Way.

Although this was stiled and waymarked by the County Council it was designed as a commercial venture by a firm providing holiday packages, which are apparently popular mainly with visitors from abroad. Edric the Wild lost his five manors to the invading Normans in spite of boldly besieging Shrewsbury in 1069.

The ODP goes up through a new planting of conifers and then over a stile into the more mature Churchtown Wood, which is mainly deciduous. The path goes steeply up through the wood but the surface is hard. *The considerable bank of the Dyke is on the left.*

Like the previous climb the steepest part is near the bottom, and the gradient eases off, particularly when the wood is left behind. A stile leads out into an open pasture where the ODP (now with the Shropshire Way) goes along the top of a subsidiary bank with the ditch and main bank of the Dyke to the left. On the crest of Knuck [Mound] Bank a stile on the main ridge of the Dyke leads onto a road. A few yards to the right along this turn left along a grassy track with blackthorn on the left to a stile on the Dyke.

Through the next field the path starts to descend with the Dyke on the left, with a fence on the top. Soon the path is going down steeply, with spruces on the left, to a wooden footbridge. Going up again the path is on the left of the Dyke, with a fence on the left, and then crosses the Dyke, crossing a track going left to Middle Knuck Farm before going over a stile somewhat to the right. Keep to the right of a corrugated iron barn, beyond which a fence and a low stretch of the Dyke are to the left.

A stile leads to a descent into another valley, with the path back on top of the Dyke. *The large hill ahead is Hergan and the farms of*

Skeltons Bank and Cwm [Valley] are on the skyline ahead to the right.
The path switches into the ditch on the right before a stile at the
bottom and a footbridge over another stream to the right.

The stile before the climb onto the next ridge has "Eaton's
Coppice" cut into it, but this hardly seems to exist in practice although
it is shown on maps. The stile also refers to "OFFAR EX". On the
ascent there are large sycamores planted on the Dyke, under which
the path passes. At the top of the steepest climbing there is a stile in a
post and wire fence, beyond which the climbing is easier and the
Dyke higher behind a fence and a band of trees. From the stile at the
end of the next short field Cwm Farm is to the right.

The next field is almost level but does include the highest point of
this ridge for the ODP. From the next stile, which has a shapely
sycamore to the right, the way is definitely down and soon curving
to the left, following the Dyke. The ODP switches to the left of the
Dyke over a stile, with Golly Coppice over to the left. A stream is
crossed in a little dip and the path climbs again on top of the Dyke,
with the Dyke clearly turning right ahead.

*This area has provided archaeologists with some problems, as the join
of the Dyke is clumsy. The official view seems to be that two teams of dyke
builders made a mess of their alignments. What a good job they were not
building the Channel tunnel!*

Bear right with the Dyke past the intersection to a sign indicating
that the Shropshire Way turns sharp left. Our route does the same,
leaving the ODP and going in the opposite direction to Walk 6 for
about 600 yards. Go over a stile to the left of a gate across the track.
Colebatch Hill is almost straight ahead. Continue up the gravel-surfaced
track, passing a quarry on the right. Later the track is grassy but
continues to climb. When it turns sharply to the right go ahead over
a stile beside a gate. Follow the fence on the left for about 20 yards
and then take the stile to the left. Go along a grassy track with fence
and hedge on the left to a facing gate.

*The Long Mynd should be seen in the distance ahead on a clear day,
with Wenlock Edge to the right and further away. If pointed hills can be
seen over Wenlock Edge they will be Brown Clee and Titterstone Clee.*

Offa's Dyke on Edenhope Hill

After going through the gate the fence is on the right. The track goes down and through a gap into the next field, where it continues down on the right of the field to a gate in the corner. The same thing happens in the next field.

The large farm below to the right is Shadwell Hall; the hill ahead is Bryn [Hill] Hill, with Blakeridge Wood on it and Cefn Einion beneath it. To the right a view is opening up along the River Unk.

In the last field Shadwell Hall is across a narrowing field on the right. The track bears right through a gate onto a road. Turn left along the road and soon go across a crossroads, with a sign to Cefn Einion. The road drops down to cross the River Unk on a bridge with stone parapets and then climbs up, steeply only at the end, to the crossroads in Cefn Einion.

4. Go ahead at the crossroads, passing the postbox, between houses which were once the malthouse and the smithy. *(Cefn Einion must have been an important place at one time!)* The road soon passes a turn on the left to Mainstone and then climbs with part of Blakeridge Wood on the right. From the top of the slope continue along the road as far as the way into the Forestry Commission Blakeridge Woods on the right. Ignore this an in about 100 yards, just before an isolated mountain ash tree in the hedge on the left, turn left through a gate. *(It is probably slightly quicker, if duller and little shorter, to continue on the road back to Colebatch).*

Go straight down the sloping field from the stile to a stout fence post and continue down a rough slope with a fence on the right. At the bottom, at a junction of paths, cross over the stream and join a track slanting up to the right. As indicated by waymarks, pass to the right of all the buildings at Goat House, going through a gate and across the top of a short field, with a wall on the left. To leave the field go through another gate and then cross the next field parallel to the wood on the right. *The prominent hill coming into view over the left end of Blakeridge Wood to the right is Oakeley Mynd.*

After another gate proceed in a similar fashion through the next field, on a sort of terrace. After the next gate continue through a field with a parkland feel to it. There is a fence on the right with bracken behind it. From a pair of oak trees beside the path continue along, now with a fence on the left. *By this stage the Long Mynd should be in sight over to the right.*

Go through a small dip into the next field and continue with a hedge and fence on the left, curving round to the left. After another gate there is a fence on the right. Keep along the "green lane" next to the fence if possible, otherwise keep to the left of a line of hawthorns. At the end of the field a low fence leads out onto a tarmac track. Turn right along this and keep down past a nursery to a T-junction with the road from Cefn Einion. Turn left along this and reach Colebatch in about half a mile, passing the turn on the outward route about half way.

Whitcott Keysett

A climb up to the Cefns ridge, which gives fine views across Shropshire, then an interesting section of Offa's Dyke.

Distance: 5¼ miles.

Start: *Whitcott Keysett is on the north side of the valley of the River Clun about 2 miles northwest of Clun itself. Start at the centre of the village, where a house is surrounded by a triangle of roads. Grid ref. 275 828. (Landranger 137, Pathfinder 930, Explorer 201 - 216 also needed).*

With care it is possible to park in the village without causing inconvenience.

By bus: *There is a Royal Mail Postbus route 743 from Newcastle-on-Clun on Mondays, Tuesdays and Thursdays and Horrocks Coach Travel have route 773 from Bishop's Castle on Tuesdays.*

Whitcott Keysett [White cottage of Sergeant of Police] is a small village, but it has some pleasant buildings dating from the 17th and 18th centuries.

The Route

1. Start off along the road to Mardu and Cefn Einion [Anvil Ridge], passing houses and bungalows on the left, followed by the entrance to the farm of Shukers House, which has a barn with unusual triangular ventilation holes. Very soon a waymark on the right shows the way up a grass slope to a gate into a field. Go through this and, on coming into the open field, turn right up the field aiming for a

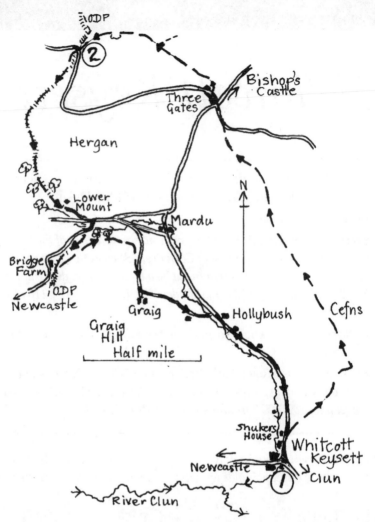

stile in the top fence which is hidden behind bushes to the left of a fenced section projecting downward into the field.

From the stile go left for a few yards across the corner of the field to another one and then keep in the same direction (to the left of the highest part of the hill). *Down to the left is a beautiful pastoral scene, much of which will be traversed on the return. Mardu [Steward's house] can be seen in the valley beyond an obvious converted chapel.*

Once over the crest (in about 150 yards) a waymarked gap should be seen in the fence coming up from a wood to the left. From the gap proceed in the direction given by the waymark, diagonally up the next field. *Behind, the valley of the River Clun can be seen beyond Whitcott Keysett, running down to Clun to the left. To the right it comes past Newcastle, and the Offa's Dyke Path (ODP) climbs up onto Spoad Hill on the far side.*

At the remains of the next hedgeline turn right, up to the top of the field and then turn left on a path (part of the Shropshire Way) which climbs up the ridge called Cefns. [Strictly Cefnen means Ridge.] It is a long gradual climb, with fine views over the fence on the right. The stile on the right very soon is a good spot to look at the view, but should not be crossed.

The ridge is too broad to see the valley of the River Unk below the ridge, but there is plenty to see beyond it. The large wood slightly to the left is Blakeridge Wood, which is passed on Walk 5. Red Wood is the next large wood to the right. Between the two and much further back may be seen the ridge of the Long Mynd.

Go up the ridge with a fence on the right on the grassy path and go through a gateway into the next section of pasture. *Looking back Clun can be seen at the confluence of the Rivers Clun and Unk.* The fence bends to the left and then, after a stile, back to the right as the path continues to rise gently beside it. After the next stile the climb is initially steeper, but the views to the east continue to improve.

The full length of the Long Mynd can now be seen on a clear day and Wenlock Edge, Brown Clee Hill and Titterstone Clee Hill may even be seen further back to the right of the Long Mynd. Down in the valley near at hand are the buildings of Llanhedric [Edric's glade] Farm.

The next stile can be seen on the skyline ahead, and from this the summit of Cefns can be seen to the right of the fence. Keep to the fence as it bends round to the right to another stile, which is beside a gate. From this bear to the left, away from the fence, descending to reach a stile in the far left corner of the field. From this stile follow the fence on the left which bears right and then, more definitely, left.

Go through a facing gate onto an grassy track, enclosed by fences. After another gate across the track there is a hedge on the right and the track bears down right towards Three Gates. Go through another gate out onto a road. Go ahead on the road, passing a farm on the right and junctions to left and right. Just before the farmhouse on the right of the road (which is built in stone but is hung with slate on the front) turn right into a track, which may be very muddy. Fight your way up through this (if no better route has been provided) to a facing gate and stile on the right after the track has turned left and widened out.

Continue on with a fence on the right up a steep slope which eases before a stile is reached. You are now, apparently, on not only the Shropshire Way but also Wild Edrik's Way! Continue across the next short field with the fence still on the right to a gate and stile at the top, passing, on the way, a stile on the right. Walk 5 goes over this after sharing the next bit of our route but in the opposite direction.

From the stile go somewhat to the left, joining a tractor track going downhill, bisecting the angle of the two fences at the corner. The track improves further down and then passes an old quarry on the left. Go over a stile on the right of a gate across the track and continue down to a fingerpost which indicates that the Shropshire Way (but not this walk) is turning back to the right, and also that we are now joining the Offa's Dyke Path (ODP).

Looking to the right Offa's Dyke can be clearly seen coming over a number of ridges from Churchtown. It turns right at a junction which has confused archaelogists. The Dyke to the north is basically straight, going over hills and ridges. That to the south, which we will be going on (probably because it was built by a different team), rather than going straight over the top of Hergan Hill, contours round the side of it, making walking less energetic. Much of it is also a fine example of the Dyke at its most defensible, with a large ridge on the left/east/Mercian side, then a deep ditch and finally a lesser bank.

2. Continue along the track to a stile and gate which lead onto a road. Cross the road to another gate and stile from which the ODP goes along the top of the Dyke, with the road initially running parallel on the left, but rising as the Dyke is going down. *Ahead is a very pleasant valley scene, with a patchwork of fields and woods.* The path goes through a band of trees, mostly sycamores with some ash, and gradually slopes down toward the valley bottom. Be careful not to take any of the tracks going left up the hill.

A stile on the line of the top bank goes over a well-laid hedge and the path then starts to bend round to the left with the slope of the hill. *In autumn there are many types of fungi here.* A descent through a scrubby wood leads to a stile and a grassy field across a small streamless valley bottom. The path then climbs again, with the Dyke avoiding the higher ground to the left, and the path most often in the ditch. Ignore a waymarked path going to the right and descend gently through a mixed wood, with some of the trees thickly encrusted with lichen, and multiple trunks indicating previous coppicing.

Eventually a stream is seen down on the right and the wood is left through a gate, leading to a path enclosed between hedges. After passing to the left of a wooden garage and the right of a house [Lower

Mardu

Mount] go down a track to a lane. Turn left along the lane and soon turn right at a junction of lanes. In about 100 yards go left over a stile which leads to a footbridge over a stream and a climb up to the right to another stile. From the stile there is a further climb up the next field, bearing right with bracken on the slope from the Dyke to a stream down to the right,

After another stile the path is level along the side of a valley to another stile after which there is a pond down on the right, but the ODP goes up left to a stile in the fence on the left before an ash tree. Bridge Farm is down the track to the right and the ODP goes across, but we turn back left along the track.

The track climbs a little at first but soon levels out after a gateway, with views to the left of the ODP skirting Hergan Hill. The track bears round to the right and there are a fence and a coppice on the left. Just before the next gate the buildings of Mardu can be seen down to the left, with Three Gates at the top of the shallow valley beyond it. Shortly after another gate, consisting mainly of corrugated iron, join a lane coming up from Mardu and take a left fork just before the farm of Graig [Rock].

The surfaced track winds down into the valley. Another track comes in from the right and a stone, wood and corrugated iron barn on the left is passed. From a newly renovated cottage [The Tump] on the right the lane goes down more steeply to a ford, where there is a footbridge on the right. Go right at the junction with a road, which is followed to the right for about two thirds of a mile back to Whitcott Keysett, accompanied by a stream on the right.

The first farm on the left is Hollybush and then there is an old cottage on the right with incongruous continental-style window shutters in pale blue. The next house on the left is more traditional and then there is a converted chapel, also on the left. After another farm on the right the outward route is rejoined just before Shukers House.

Knucklas

The walk passes over the historic Castle Hill to Lloyney, and then crosses the River Teme. Mainly quiet roads lead up to a fine stretch of Offa's Dyke above the Teme Valley on the return leg.

Distance: *9¼ miles, with an extra ½ mile to visit the top of Castle Hill.*

Start: *The start of the walk is by the telephone box and postbox on the north of the stream over the brook at the west end of Knucklas village. Grid ref. 251 742 (Landranger 148, Pathfinder 950, Explorer 201). There is limited parking near here, but the widest road is that coming into the village from the east.*

By public transport: *The obvious route to Knucklas is by train, on the Heart of Wales line which runs from Shrewsbury (via Knighton) to Llandrindod Wells and Swansea. To get to the starting point from the station go down to the road through the village, turn left and fork right at the Castle Inn. Turn right over a bridge to a telephone box. There is also a bus service from Knighton, the G5, run by Sargeant Brothers.*

Knucklas (Green Mound) has a long history, some of it shrouded in myth. Much of this is based on Cnwclas Castle , which may have been the site of the wedding of King Arthur and Queen Guinevere. Guinevere is fabled to have been the daughter of a local chieftain, a giant called Gogyrfan and it may have been from here that Arthur set out to free Britain from Saxon rule.

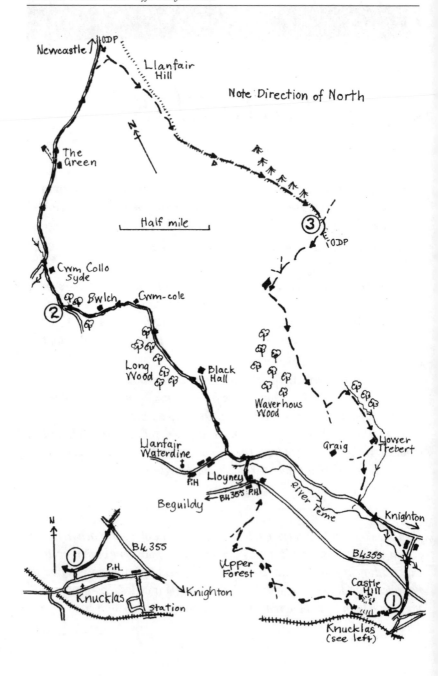

Note Direction of North

Half mile

In later times the castle was the stronghold of the Marcher Lords, the Mortimers, the last castle on the site being built about 1220 and sacked by Llywelyn the Last in 1262 and Owain Glyndwr in 1402. The only fortifications now are the mock ones (reminiscent of those on the railway tunnel adjacent to Conwy Castle, but less relevant). The railway was built about 1883, some of the stone being from Castle Hill. The viaduct now dominates the village which has the Castle Inn, but no shop.

The Route

1. *(Note that a little distance and quite a bit of climbing can be avoided by taking the road route to Lloyney, but the chance of going up Castle Hill and some good views would be missed.)* Go up the lane with the post box and telephone box on the left. This climbs to get first level with and then above the railway, which is close by on the left. On the right are houses, one of which, The Old Shop, hints at a more generally useful past. Beyond the houses, on the lower slopes of Castle Hill, there are rock faces, with a shaly stone (officially Upper Silurian siltstones and shales) which splits into layers. The rocks are followed by a lot of Dog Rose bushes, which must be a fine sight in June and July.

Bend round to the right with the road and continue to climb steeply up to Bwthyn Castell [Castle Cottage]. Continue ahead with a footpath sign, passing a track down to the left, to reach a farm building with a semicylindrical corrugated iron roof. If you wish to visit the site of Cnwclas Castle keep to the right of the building, otherwise turn left.

The route to the castle climbs up a track, goes through a gate and turns right at a T-junction of paths. Keep rising on a grassy path with blackthorn on the right and bear right through a gate, with a quarry ahead, where a sign indicates that this is only a permissive path. Climb up to the right of the quarry to the humps and bumps of the fortifications. Rather than tackle the steep path ahead bear round to the left, and keep below the bank on the right to reach a descriptive plaque.

Continue round the bank, in which a section of the original wall can be seen, to a large pit (from which stone has presumably been quarried) and go up to the top level at this point, which was the original entrance of the last castle on the site. *This was built in 1220-5 by Hugh Mortimer II and destroyed in 1262 by the Welsh Llywellyn ap Gruffydd in his rebellion. With a bit of imagination it is possible to see the positions of the four corner turrets, but the finest thing is the view in all directions, up, across and down the Teme Valley and also up the other little valleys which converge at Knucklas.* To return to the route retrace your steps to the farm building and turn right.

Whether or not the castle has been visited go immediately to the left of the corrugated iron-roofed building into a field and go up the field with a fence on the left. At the top of the field look briefly back to see the castle remains more clearly than "on the spot". Go through the gate, turn right briefly and then curve round left on a track, with a hedge on the right. The track goes through a gate and continues to climb with hedges and fences on both sides. From the crest the track descends slightly, goes through a gate, bears right and rises slightly again.

To the left Red Wood covers a hillside and to the right, across the Teme Valley, is Trebert Wood, with the Offa's Dyke Path (ODP) crossing the hills behind it. The hill to the right of Trebert Wood is Cwm-sanahan, which is traversed on Walk 8, and this present walk will return over Llanfair [Church of St Mary] Hill further to the left. The hill ahead, covered in bracken, with a green track climbing it, is Goytre [House in wood] Hill.

The track descends more steeply, goes through another gate and bends left. At a junction of tracks, with farm buildings ahead, turn right. *The village of Lloyney [Bushes], to which we are heading, can be seen in the valley ahead.* The farmhouse of Upper Forest Farm on the left is soon passed, with fine roses on its front. The lane bears round to the right and then swings sharply right to go down the left hand side of a shallow valley. Join another lane coming in from the left and pass a bungalow and Hobby Farm below on the right, over which there is a fine view down the broad valley of the Teme. Pass more buildings on either side before reaching the B4355 at a T-junction.

Turn left through the village of Lloyney, passing three houses on the right and the Lloyney Inn on the left. Turn right past the 300 year old Lloyney Mill, on the road signposted to Llanfair Waterdine [St Mary's Church by the Water]. Pass into Shropshire and go over the fast flowing River Teme. Turn left at a T-junction and climb to a junction with farm tracks. Turn right here towards Black Hall.

This bypasses the village of Llanfair Waterdine, whose main attractions (both at the far end of the village) are the Red Lion and St Mary's Church. This is a Victorian structure, but contains a few older things. The altar rail was made from the finely (and most interestingly) carved old rood screen of about 1600, and the pew ends are painted with the names of local farms. There is also an old font, supposedly Saxon. The destruction of the old church was described by a church archaeologist as ".. one of the most wicked cases of vandalism I have ever come across".

The lane towards Black Hall soon descends with Waverhouse Wood ahead. Do not go through a gate on the right which is actually a bridleway, but keep left, with a stream down on the right accompanying the lane. The lane starts to climb with hedges on each side composed mainly of hazel and hawthorn, with some wild roses. When the lane splits, with the right fork going to Black Ball, keep left again, climbing slightly. *The valley, woods and hills behind Black Hall make a fine picture to the right when they can be seen through gaps in the hedge.*

Continue along the lane, soon with Long Wood on the left and a hedge on the right. The lane bends left and the wood on the left is replaced by an open, brackeny slope, with occasional trees and gorse. The buildings of Cwm-cole to the right are passed. (One has a date of 1991 on it, presumably relating to a renovation.) The lane now curves left again and starts to climb. On the col are the buildings of Bwlch [Pass], the farmhouse itself a ruin. The lane winds down through a wood, with more of the shaly rock apparent on the right, and meets a road coming in from the left.

2. Go right along the road, which soon bends left and then right. The road rises a little and then drops down to Cwm Collo Syde. Pass the farm, cross over a stream and turn right at a T-junction, with a sign to Springhill, Newcastle and Clun. This road will now be followed for about 1¼ miles, most of it uphill, but the steepest part will soon be dealt with. The road passes back over a branch of the stream and turns left to climb steeply. *On the right more of the shaly stone is being washed away, leaving tree roots in the air.* After a right hand bend the ridge on the right can be seen, where the Offa's Dyke Path (ODP) will form part of the return leg of the walk.

After a fairly level stretch a bungalow (The Green) on the right and a track on the left are passed, at the midpoint of the climb. *A fine view is developing behind, with Beacon Hill to the right of Pool Hill and Wernygeufron [Marsh of the enclosed hillside] Hill lower and further to the left.* The road has only wire fences at the sides further up and so the views are better, particularly of the ridge to the right and the valley of the Teme behind. At the crest of the hill a track goes right, which is a short cut to the ODP, (joining the ODP by turning right when there is a gate ahead). For reasons which may become apparent in Volume 5 this walk drops slightly to where an ODP fingerpost shows a path cutting back sharply to the right.

Climb on this path and, on joining the track from the road crest, go ahead along it. The stony track climbs with wire fences at the sides and goes through a gate. Llanfair Hill is on the left, with Offa's Dyke obvious below it and merging with our track. After two dips, interleaved with two more gates, the Dyke is immediately on the left. The ODP turns left over a stile and then continues on top of the Dyke.

There is now a fine view over to the left down a shallow valley to the wooded Sunnyhill and Radnor Wood beyond Clun [Moor], with Rock Hill and Cefn Hepreas to the right and nearer. This is a splendid section of the Dyke, which is a really impressive earthwork. There was a notice to the effect that the reason that the ODP is not always on top of the Dyke is for preservation purposes, and along this stretch the path has worn into the surface by up to a foot.

Level with a trig point to the right (an endangered species now that surveying is done from the air) the ODP goes over another stile. *This, at over 1,400 feet, is the highest point on Offa's Dyke (although the ODP gets much higher).* The path hardly seems to drop as it continues along the Dyke and there are stiles on each side of the track we had used earlier, as it cuts through to the left of the Dyke. Soon there is a small plantation of mixed conifers on the left and as the ODP descends beside it there is a stile over a wire fence to be climbed.

Soon a track leading to a corrugated iron barn is crossed and, just before the next stile, the Dyke is riddled with the entrances to a badger sett (doing much more damage than human feet!) From the stile a right of way goes down to the right into the valley, the view along which is now opening up. The descent on the ODP is accompanied by conifers, initially on the left. After a stile the path goes down among larches, with the gradient increasing after another stile and another badger sett are negotiated. After the last of the larches the path drops down to a track.

3. *Walk 8 comes in from the left at this point.* Go through the gate to the right and continue, now with the Dyke on the left. At the corner of the fence on the right we leave the ODP (after a particularly fine section of Offa's Dyke itself) by turning right and proceeding with the fence and hawthorn trees on the right. The path climbs slightly to a gate in the corner of the field and soon after that begins to drop, still with the fence on the right, to another gate in the next field corner. Continue to descend beside the fence and hedge which curve round to another gate. Go beside a stream on the left very briefly, but then bear right to a gate in a fence, beside a clump of trees.

The gatepost has a plethora of waymarks on it. Our way is through the gate and then left on a track which passes to the left of extensive farm buildings. After the buildings turn left through an unusually wide gate, on a hard surfaced track. *The fence on the left soon has something akin to a motorway barrier as its bottom section.* After this the track becomes an enclosed lane. Another track comes in from the right, through a gate beneath an ash tree. At a gateway continue ahead with a bridleway sign and also an indication that we are on the Jack Mytton Way (a 72 mile bridleway through Shropshire from Billingsley to Llanfair Waterdine).

Very soon turn left down a metalled lane and then turn right in the valley bottom through a gate before reaching the stream. Head to the left of some trees ahead and proceed with a line of trees on the right and a fence on the left, beyond which are the stream and a wood. At the end of this stretch go through a facing gate with a waymark on the post. The next stretch may be overgrown with nettles, but leads to Lower Trebert.

Go between the buildings and turn right on a track which soon goes over a cattle grid. Keep on the track to a line of trees, and then, instead of going right on the track to Graig [Rock] Farm, turn left towards a gate in a crossing fence. *Trebert Wood is to the left, across a small valley.* In the next field descend towards Castle Hill, passing a succession of isolated trees, the first of which is a hollow-centred ash. At the bottom of the field a gate leads out onto a road, along which you should turn left.

The road bends left and there is a fine example of an ox-bow lake below on the right, the remains of a previous line of the River Teme. Turn in through the next gate on the right and aim for the right hand end of the buildings of Monaughty Poeth farm, keeping the river on the right. *It was near Monaughty Poeth that the skeletons of five tall men were found during the excavation of a mound. The find has been associated with the King Arthur legend.*

From the edge of the farm continue near the river to a gate which leads onto a road. Turn right along the road and almost immediately cross the River Teme. Continue to a T-junction (with the B4355). Turn left here and very soon right to return to the start of the walk in about 300 yards.

Five Turnings

Gentle pastoral scenery along the valley of the River Redlake, then a climb up to follow Offa's Dyke above the Teme Valley over Cwm-sanahan Hill.

Distance: *6¼ miles.*

Start: *At Five Turnings, about 3 miles north of Knighton on the A488 towards Clun. Grid ref. 286 754 (Landranger 148, Pathfinder 950, Explorer 201). There is room for parking about 200 yards down the side road, outside a scrapyard (if you want to risk it!) but probably better is on the side road that the walk turns into very soon, which is initially quite wide. There are also some possible parking spots in Purlogue, but care should be taken not to obstruct access to fields or farm machinery.*

By bus: *There are no bus services which give sufficient time to do the walk.*

Five Turnings is little more than a road junction. Three of the "turnings" are roads and two bridleways, but there is a mysterious third bridleway, which seems to exist only on the map.

The Route

1. From Five Turnings head north (towards Clun and away from Knighton) on the A488 for nearly half a mile. *(There is a decent verge on the right to walk on when traffic threatens.)* Turn left into a side road with a signpost pointing to Purlogue [Enclosure by the gate]. After a new bungalow on the right the lane narrows. Soon keep left when a track goes right to Purlogue Farm over a cattle grid. *Purlogue is in* *the valley ahead, with Rock Hill behind to the right and Cefn Hepreas to the left. An unusual sight on the right soon is a tree which appears to be half holly, half hawthorn, the trunks having fused together.*

As the lane descends the hedges get higher and it winds past The White House and the drive to Lloiney [Bushes] Farmhouse on the left. When the lane levels out a stream is crossed and the road through the valley is met at a T-junction, where the route goes left. *Purlogue is little more than a succession of farms in the valley of the River Redlake, which is occasionally seen on the right as it heads east to join the River Clun in about seven miles.*

Pass Field Farm on the right and Green Farm on the left and a turn to the left, where the route continues along the valley. Pass a bungalow on the right and turn left onto a tarmacked track just before a white house on the left. The track goes up a steepening slope towards Back Wood and then bears right to reach a road. (The direct route is full of brambles and definitely not recommended.)

At the road turn sharp left, and then turn right through a gate onto a bridleway which goes up a groove on the edge of Back Wood. After the wood is left behind the bridleway continues to climb in its groove and the view steadily opens up. *Over to the left, beyond a nearby wood, the trees on the horizon are on Cwm-sanahan Hill. Further round to the left, on the right of the Redlake valley is Caer Caradoc [Caractacus's Castle], with Hodre Hill on its left, across the valley.*

A track comes in from the right and the groove becomes less obvious and the slope less steep as the climb progresses. *(Presumably this was once a hedged "green lane", but now few of the trees remain from the hedges.)* Beyond a ruined building go ahead through a gate. *If you look directly back the wood on the horizon is on Black Hill.* Continue ahead, with a fence and line of trees on the right, to a fence at the top of the hill. *There is a fine view ahead across the Teme Valley. Directly across the valley is Wernygeufron [Marsh of the enclosed hillside] Hill. The hills to the left of it above the Teme are traversed on Walks 7 and 9.*

Turn right through a gate and climb slightly with a fence on the left. Once over the crest of the hill bend left with the fence. *To the*

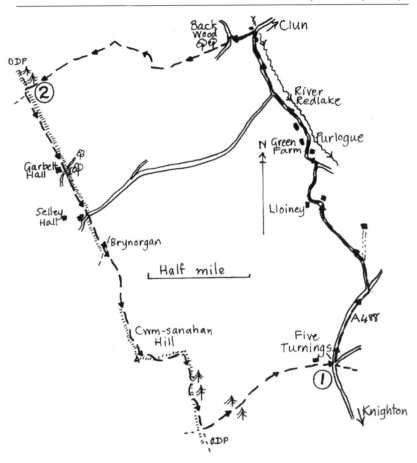

right are Cefn Hepreas and Rock Hill (with trees in its hollows), now close at hand. Llanfair [Church of St Mary] Hill is further away to the left of Cefn Hepreas. Continue with the fence on the left through a slight dip to a gate in the corner of the field. Go through the gate or over the adjacent stile and continue with a fence (and soon a hedge) on the left. *Cwm-sanahan Hill is now looming large on the horizon to the left.*

At the end of the field go through a facing gate and bear to the left in the next field to reach a gate in the crossing hedge near the corner of the field. The gate out of the next field is next to the hedge on the left. Keep near the fence on the left to rendezvous with Walk 7 and a line of larches coming down on and around the prominent bank of Offa's Dyke to the right.

2. At this point the Offa's Dyke Path (ODP) is joined. Go left through the gateway and continue on a track with the Dyke on the left, with a high bank and deep ditch. *Ahead the line of the Dyke can be seen clearly climbing Cwm-sanahan Hill, but there is a lot of height to be lost, alas, before we get there.* The track passes through a gate into the next field. When it splits keep close to the Dyke, even on the path through the gorse if this is possible. At the bottom of the slope keep to the left of the farmhouse of Garbett Hall and go through the gate onto a lane.

Cross the lane to a stile into woods, descend to a wooden bridge over a stream and climb up to a stile. From this the path goes through bracken, soon bearing left onto the Dyke and goes down to another footbridge. From that follow the waymarks up to a stile which leads into an area of gorse, where the path climbs steadily on the Dyke. *Across the valley here is Selley Hall, a pleasant looking three-storey stone house.* Later, as waymarked, go off the Dyke to the right and go down a steeply sloping field to a stile on the line of the Dyke.

The stile leads onto a lane. *If the thought of climbing Cwm-sanahan Hill is too daunting, going left along the lane will lead back to the road through Purlogue (provided a right fork is taken).* To continue on the ODP turn left along the lane for a few yards and then go right over a stile or through a gate onto a track which goes down to the bottom of the field and then climbs up the other side to a stile and gate in the top corner. A short level stretch leads past the right of a white house, Brynorgan, to a gate and stile.

From here the path climbs steeply through a mixture of bracken, gorse and heather, but soon the path bears right, which makes it less steep. *To the right Knucklas with its railway viaduct and, on its right, the historic Castle Hill (see Walks 7 and 9) can be seen in the valley.* When the gorse is left behind the worst of the climbing is over. From a stile the path continues to climb and soon has a fence on the left, and only a slight incline. From the next stile the way to the summit is clear, along the Dyke up a slight slope.

The summit of Cwm-sanahan Hill is a magnificent viewpoint, as the land falls away steeply except to the northeast. There are fine views along the Teme Valley in both directions. To the right it stretches out past Lloyney [Bushes] and Llanfair Waterdine [St Mary's Church by the Water] towards Newtown. To the left there are fine meanders (seen most clearly from this height) in the river before Knighton. Looking across the valley, on a clear day Great Rhos [Moor] in Radnor Forest may be seen to the left of Knucklas. In the opposite direction the wooded Black Hill is still the most prominent object.

(Note that the route of the ODP may have altered slightly from that described here and shown on the map, but it will be clearly waymarked.)

On Cwm-sanahan Hill the Dyke does a right-angled turn to the left, to avoid the steep drop into the cwm. Leave the summit over another stile and descend to the top of a line of pines through which the path descends, with larches also in evidence. At a stile the path

Lunch beside the Dyke near Selley Hall

bends right. (Avoid the bridleway going down steeply into the valley to the right). The ODP climbs with a fence on the left, to regain some of the lost height.

With a sea of gorse down to the right the path goes down again to cross a subsidiary valley (with another stile in the dip and again goes up again, with an unfenced conifer plantation on the left. *The Dyke can just be made out among the trees on the left.* At the end of the wood the ODP resumes its position on top of the Dyke and climbs slightly again before dropping down to a crossing track, with Panpunton Hill ahead. (Walk 9 comes up the valley on this track and then turns right along the ODP.)

This walk leaves the ODP and the Dyke at this point, turning left along the track. When the track bears left continue ahead, with a fence on the right and a line of hawthorns on the left. Go through a facing gate and continue down, now with a larch plantation on the left. When the fence bears right (with more larches behind it) continue ahead with an intermittent path, heading to the right of a black barn. *The scrapyard on the road from Five Turnings can easily be picked out in front, with Caer Caradoc rising behind it.*

When the path veers right continue on down into the far left corner of the field (beyond Newhouse Farm to the left), where a rather damp extension to the field leads down to a gate. From this the path continues, basically as a green lane with a fence on the right, bending right before it returns to Five Turnings.

Knighton and Knucklas

The walk is flatter than some, with only one stiff climb. It goes along the ridge on the south of the Teme Valley, crosses over through Knucklas and returns along the Dyke on the north of the valley.

Distance: 7¼ miles.

Start: By the clock tower in Knighton, at the junction of Broad Street, West Street and High Street. Grid ref. 286 723 (Landranger 148, Pathfinder 950, Explorer 201). The main car park is lower down Broad Street, but there are places where it may be possible to park free, notably on Market Street, soon after the start of the walk and at the TIC and Offa's Dyke Centre .

By train or bus: Knighton is on the Heart of Wales rail line between Swansea and Shrewsbury. (From the station head up into the town and turn right at Broad Street.) There is a limited bus service from Felindre on Thursdays operated by Owens Motors. There is a better service from Ludlow and Leintwardine (numbers 738 & 740, run by Shropshire Link) and from Presteigne (Service G5, run by Sargeant Brothers).

As the point where Offa's Dyke crossed the River Teme, Knighton was bound to become a place of some importance. It is thought that the knights of its name might have been the riders who patrolled the Dyke, and its Welsh name of Tref-y-Clawdd [Town on the Dyke] is an even more direct reference. Another possible derivation of the name is as a corruption of Cnwc-din [Black Mound].

A Saxon town originally grew in the triangle between the Teme, the Wilcombe Brook and the Dyke. Later the Normans built two castles here, but the position on the borders led to attacks (successful to varying degrees) by the Welsh in 1052, 1213, 1260, 1262, and finally, by Owain Glyndwr, in 1402. The church, dedicated (uniquely in Wales) to the English king and martyr Edward, is at the bottom of Church Street. The tower and the foundations of the walls are Norman.

Another historical link is the Autumn Market, which dates from the time of Henry III. At one time wives were sold at it - a far cry from the present decorous weekly market in High Street. The clock tower of 1872 has older buildings around it. Lying back from High Street near the clock is a house with a 17th century black and white frontage and a mediaeval hall behind the adjacent shop. Across High Street in the other direction the bottom shop was originally a town house of the Brydges family, but much of it was demolished when West Street was built. Across Broad Street from the clock the building with the copper cupola, originally a bank, dates from 1904.

The Route

1. Start by going up High Street, which soon becomes The Narrows, with a mixture of tourist and local shops. At the top turn right into Market Street, which soon turns left and broadens out. Where Market Street narrows again, a few steps to the left along Plough Road will disclose the Fire Station. *The mound behind it is the site of a Norman motte and bailey Castle.*

Further along Market Street are old cottages on the left, shortly before the junction of Penybont Road and Offa's Road is reached. *(This is also the A488 to Llandrindod Wells.)* Turn left along Penybont Road, passing The Laurels, which dates from the 1830s. It is possible to see a short section of Offa's Dyke by turning left on the footpath beyond The Laurels and keeping left, behind the council houses. The Dyke can be seen over the hedge to the left behind The Laurels.

Return to the A488, cross it and turn left along the footway. Cross Radnor Drive and turn right on a footpath halfway to Garth Lane. The footpath passes between gardens to a parking area. At the end

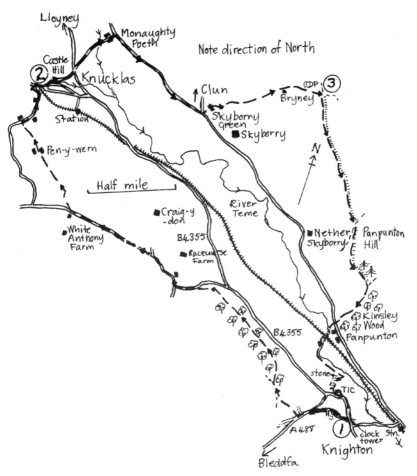

of this turn left up a tarmac path with steps, with a terrace of houses on the left. Turn right at the top onto a path and soon turn left to climb steps between rose bay willow herb up to a waymarked stile. From this the path slopes upward across the field diagonally to the right.

Across the valley of the River Teme to the right, the large wood above Knighton is Kinsley Wood, and the higher hill to the left of it is Panpunton Hill, over which the walk returns to Knighton. In the valley there are roads on each side of the river and the Heart of Wales railway line.

The path continues on and up into an area of bracken, entering a wood with trees large and small when a path comes in from the left. Almost immediately fork right on the lower of two paths and soon go through another area of bracken with larger, older trees down the slope to the right. Our path is joined by another coming up from the right and enters the old coppiced wood. *Occasionally there are glimpses of the B4355 below to the right.*

On the path (which is more or less level across a steep slope down to the right) go over or past two stiles, after the second of which there is a fence on the right. Continue along the clear path, ignoring any paths leading off to the right. *(Many of the hedges hereabouts look like properly laid "living fences", but are in fact made of loose branches. It will be interesting to see how well they last.) There are occasional fine views to the right across the Teme Valley.* Beyond a stile the path bends to the left and eventually climbs slightly, with a road below on the right. *A farm glimpsed across to the right is Racecourse Farm, for reasons which will become clear.*

Eventually join the road, climbing and then going right at a road junction with a grass triangle, continuing to climb. Pass some houses on the right and then bear left over a cattle grid where a lane to Craig-y-don [Lay-land Rock] goes right. The road, now unfenced, passes up through a common. *There was a racecourse on the top of this at least until 1870. It is now a tangle of rough grass, bracken, gorse and bramble. To the left there is now a fine view of country which is traversed by Glyndwr's Way. The prominent hill to the left, topped by a communication mast, is Garth [Enclosure] Hill and it overlooks Knighton.*

Opposite the gates into White Anthony Farm on the left leave the road by bearing right on a grassy track between the bracken, climbing to a fingerpost on the horizon. This points the way over a stile beside a gate and along the left hand side of a field to another stile beside a gate. From this stile bear diagonally left to another stile which soon comes into view and keep the same direction across the corner of the next field to a gate.

From the gate there is a beautiful view. Knucklas is below, with its prominent railway viaduct, and Castle Hill behind it. Further to the left, and much higher is the bracken covered Goytre Hill, between the valleys of the Ffrwdwen [White Torrent] Brook (to the left) and the River Teme. The most prominent hill to the right of Knucklas is Cwm-sanahan Hill, which is traversed on Walk 8. Panpunton Hill is further to the right.

The path continues in the same line down the rough slope to the far left corner. Here a stile over a fence leads to a "green lane" between coppiced trees. This leads to a stile just above a white house (Pen-y-wern [Alder Head]). Turn left along the lane from Pen-y-wern and right at a T-junction with a narrow road. This winds downwards, eventually coming to another T-junction, beside the railway viaduct. Turn right again, under the viaduct, soon taking a left fork and turn left at the next junction over a bridge crossing the combined Ffrwdwen and King's Brooks.

2. *Knucklas is described in Walk 7, which begins at the telephone box and post box on the left. Looking back the mock fortifications on the viaduct look like the ramparts of a vast castle looming over the trees.* Go on the road ahead, leaving the 30 mph zone, and curve left beneath Castle Hill. At the B4355 go left and immediately right on a road which soon crosses the River Teme and leaves Powys to enter Shropshire. Go between the buildings of Monaghty Poeth and turn right at a T-junction towards Skyborry [Granges] Green.

The road is followed for the next ¾ mile, to Skyborry Green. *Fortunately most of the traffic along the valley follows the road on the other side. The road is neatly hedged for the most part.* At the junction with the road to Clun turn left, not up the road but up the track which goes off to the right of it, to the farm of Skyborry Green. The track goes up between the buildings. When it forks keep to the left of the stone-built house and barn and keep to the obvious track as it climbs past various gates.

Just before a prominent pair of trees (oak and ash) is a good spot to catch one's breath and have a look along the valley - to the right to Knucklas and to the left towards Knighton over the river which meanders in the manner of a geography textbook—or even a geography teacher if you were unlucky! The next farm in that direction is Skyborry, and Nether Skyborry is further on still, beyond a pleasantly varied collection of trees.

Pass another small communications mast (or, possibly, a television aerial) after which the gradient eases a little. *Cwm-sanahan Hill is to the left.* Go through the facing gate beside the whitewashed house of Bryney, and then bear left to reach a track junction. Take the stony track going uphill steeply with the remains of a wall and a fence on the left. Bear right away from these near a group of crab apple trees. The gradient eases again when the track bears left. Acorn waymarks indicate where the Offa's Dyke Path (ODP) crosses the track. Walk 8 comes from the left and turns left to go along "our" track. We turn right over a stile.

3. *Offa's Dyke is prominent here as a ridge topped with stumps.* The path is to the right of the Dyke, and the Teme Valley is below to the right, but usually out of sight because of the convex slope of the hill. *When I was last there a JCB was at work removing trees and digging a ditch for a cable. What would Offa's navvies have given for such a tool? On the other hand, imagining how big a job building the Dyke would have been even with JCBs makes one realise what a vast project it was with just manual labour.*

The ODP climbs gently with the occasional stile up to a group of dying larch trees on the left of the path, on Skyborry Spur, near the highest point on the walk. The path continues on the right of the Dyke, which sometimes has a fence on top. *On a clear day it may be possible to see Great Rhos in Radnor Forest behind the hills across the valley, and even the Black Mountain beyond Hay-on-Wye further round to the left.*

On the descent Knighton comes into sight only intermittently. The Dyke and the ODP bear right to avoid the summit of Panpunton Hill and begin to descend more steeply; the Dyke also becomes steadily less significant. It is necessary to leave it briefly when it has been colonised by gorse bushes. *Looking back Knucklas and its viaduct are now beyond the meanders of the Teme. At the best viewpoint for Knighton there is a seat dedicated to the memory of Frank Noble, a local teacher and historian who was a great advocate of the ODP. There is also a monument to Roy Waters, Chairman of the Trefyclawdd 1970 Society for 10 years.*

From here keep close to the fence to reach the next stile and then keep along the top of the Dyke between a fence and the gorse. An initially grassy slope then leads down to a wood on the left and a stony track is crossed. Ahead is the mass of Kinsley Wood, but before it is reached a fingerpost shows the way down to the right to a grassy track between the bracken. Further down the track is more tightly confined between bracken and gorse, and trees start to appear beside the path as well.

Shortly before the Skyborry road is reached, the path bends left, and it is seen that the path is now below the level of Knighton - so more climbing will be needed! A gate leads out onto the road and there is a stile directly opposite. From this a path leads down to a fingerpost on the bank of the River Teme. Go left here, cross the railway line on a foot crossing and then turn right to cross a footbridge over the river. (The springs on the gates on each side of the bridge are very convenient.)

A path now leads left, with the river on the left. *The river is clearly cutting into the stony subsoil on a bend.* Leave the field by a kissing gate beside the river, leading onto a paved path beside an amazingly bent willow tree. After two more kissing gates the path paving disappears and there is higher ground on the right. A sign welcomes us back to Wales and we soon turn right up a set of steps into a meadow. Cross this to the far right corner where there is a plaque commemorating Offa's Dyke beside the bank, which is (of course) Offa's Dyke. To see more of it and the stone and plaques commemorating the opening of the Offa's Dyke Park and the ODP go to the right through the Dyke and turn right along the Dyke to the end of the field.

Retrace your steps and go up the ramp onto the top level field, where there is a splendid children's playground. Ignore this and go to the right of the new Offa's Dyke Centre, which replaced the previous one in an old primary school in 1998. *(This is a fine source of information about the ODP, the Dyke and the local area.)* Turn left along West Street to return to the start of the walk.

Whitton

The River Lugg and historic Pilleth are followed by pleasant countryside and a climb up to a fine elevated section of Offa's Dyke over Hawthorn Hill.

Distance: *7½ miles. (This can be done as separate walks of 5½ and 3¼ miles by walking along the B4357 to the north of Whitton.)*

Start: *At the main crossroads in Whitton. Grid ref. 272 672. (Landranger 137, Pathfinder 971, Explorer 201.) There is room to park by the roadside near the church, and also on the Knighton road near the crossroads.*

By bus: *The only useful bus serving Whitton is the G17 from Knighton and New Radnor run by Sargeant Brothers.*

Whitton is a small village, mostly of modern houses, but the mill was referred to in a document of 1356 and the village in one of 1563. The school opened in 1724 as a result of a legacy from a certain Dame Anna Child. Part of the present building was erected in 1894, but it has been extended recently, including a fine hall now used as a village hall.

The church of St David is Victorian and later, but contains a 14th century font, an earlier stoup and a monument of 1597 which were originally in the church at Pilleth until that was burnt down in 1894. The churchyard is circular, indicating an ancient foundation. The derivation of the name may be "Hwita's farm" or "white settlement".

The Route

1. From the crossroads take the road going downhill opposite to the one to Knighton. This is the B4357 and has a weight limit sign for Whitton Bridge. Litton Hill is ahead as the road descends. The house

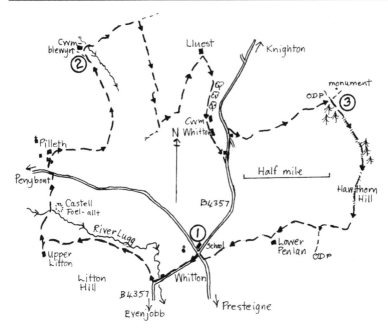

Bridge End is on the right just before the River Lugg is crossed on the road bridge. Immediately after the bridge turn right on a bridleway, with a small quarry on the left. The stony track (with grass down the middle) rises a little and then contours around the lower slopes of Litton Hill, with the treelined River Lugg meandering below to the right. Go over a cattle grid and enter an enclosed track with no views, but a hedge pleasantly threaded with honeysuckle in season.

A gate leads out into an open field. Keep on the main track when a less used bridleway goes to the left and then branch right as indicated across the grass before reaching Upper Litton Farm. Turn right again, go ahead through the right of two gates and then go down the field with a hedge on the left. Cross the Lugg again on a concrete slab bridge, pass through a gate and go uphill on a grassy track. *The mound on the right is Castell Foel-allt [Woodhill Castle], with clear remains of its motte and large bailey overlooking the river.* After the mound the track has small trees on the left (mainly hawthorn) and, later, a fence and stream on the right.

Ahead is Pilleth [Pool slope], which, unusually for anywhere in Wales, is mentioned in Domesday Book. The mainly white building to the left is Pilleth Court, parts of which date from about 1600. The church, lying further up Bryn Glas [Green Hill] to the left, was originally mediaeval, when it was a place of pilgrimage. Except for the tower it was rebuilt in 1894 after a fire destroyed it. (To judge from the wooden supports it is in a poor state again now.) A holy well behind the church is reputed to have miraculous properties.

Pilleth's main claim to fame is as the site of Owain Glyndwr's first significant victory over the English in 1402. Although the Ordnance Survey show the site of the battle on the south of the road it is thought that it was fought on the slopes of Bryn Glas, with Edmund Mortimer's English troops charging up the hill and being (so it is said) mown down by Mortimer's own Welsh archers. Many bones were discovered as recently as the 19th century.

Go through a gate onto the B4356 road, turn left for a short distance and then turn right up the bridleway to Pilleth Court Farm. Go between the first of the farm buildings, with the farmhouse to the left. The way out is to the right beyond the farm buildings on a bridleway labelled Cwm-blewyn, but it is possible to visit the church (not usually open) by turning left before a wooden barn. To continue go through the gateway at the top of the farmyard and bear right on a good metalled track over a cattle grid. The track climbs gently but steadily. There is a barn on the left and then a windbreak line of trees on the right. *As the climb continues the view over the Lugg Valley to the right improves. Whitton can be seen below and Upper Litton can be seen further to the right, below the summit of Llan-fawr [Greatchurch]. Further to the right still is Bryn Glas, fringed with conifers.*

As the gradient eases off go over another cattle grid and bear left with the track. Go through a gateway. *The steep valley below on the right is Cwm Blewyn [Hairs Valley].* After the next gate the track is fenced and Rhos [Moor] Hill is ahead. Go through another gate, with the farmhouse of Cwm-blewyn in sight ahead, but before the farm turn right and cross the culverted stream with a small pond on the right.

Walking beside the earthworks of Castell Foel-allt towards Pilleth

2. The track goes through a gate and bears left to climb a short but steep hill. At the top of the climb ignore a track on the left, instead go ahead through a gate into an area of sheep pens including a "sheep shower". (Is this a safer form of sheep dip?) Leave the area by another gate and go ahead on a stony fenced track. Before the next gate across the track turn right through a gate and down a stony track with grass down the middle and a fence on the left. Go through a gap into the next field, at the end of which go through two gates, with a corrugated iron barn on the right. Again continue with the fence on the left and bear right at the end of the field to a further gate on the left.

Turn left with the track here through the gate and go down the middle of a meadow. Go through a gateway into the next field. (The right of way in the next field is complicated. Unless waymarks have been put in follow these instructions as closely as you can.) Continue with a fence on the right until it bears away to the right. Continue in the same direction for about 30 yards and then turn back left across the field, keeping away from the fence on the right, even after it zigzags towards you. Once over the crest of the hill aim for the lowest corner of the field ahead and go through the gate there.

Witton Church

Turn left on the stony track. *A small quarry can be seen on Cwm-Whitton Hill across the valley to the right.* Follow the track, ignoring a gate on the left, with a hedge on the left and go through a gate in a crossing hedge which comes up from the valley to the right. Go through the next field parallel to the hedge on the left and again go through a gate in a crossing hedge. From here go along the hedge on the right, which slants down towards the valley to reach Lluest [Tent] Farm in the corner of the field.

Having left the field, head towards a brick bungalow, but before reaching it go right through a gate and head across the field towards a track climbing the hillside opposite. In the far left corner of the field go through the right of two gates and go through the next field to a gate in sight with a wood on the left. *The wood is, still accurately, called The Werns [Alder Trees].* Keep the fence on the left to Cwm Whitton Farm. Level with the first farm buildings, go ahead through a metal field gate and keep ahead through the farm. After the farm the stony farm track rises for a short time between fences and then drops to pass a pair of cottages and reach the B4357.

A quick return to Whitton may be made by turning right, but to continue the recent zigzag route turn left along the road, which is quite a busy one at times. Pass a road on the right which is "Unsuitable for heavy goods vehicles" and the bungalow "Cwmway" with its pretty garden. Turn right through the next gate onto a stony track which passes behind the bungalow and heads towards a little valley but bears left before reaching it. When the track splits continue up with the valley on the right to a gate in a crossing fence. From this follow the faint track which goes up the slope, now slanting left, away from the stream.

Eventually the gradient slackens off and the track bears left into a field corner where there are a number of gates and (rather surprisingly in view of the distance from a railway) an old railway truck. Go through the rightmost gate, now with a bridleway waymark, and go through the next upland pasture with a fence on the left. Keep close to the fence to reach a metal field gate just in front of a conifer plantation at the top of Cwm Whitton Hill. Turn left and then right to get to the other side of this.

3. Here our route turns right, joining the Offa's Dyke Path (ODP). *The stone obelisk in the field is a memorial to the first baronet of Radnor, Sir R G Price MP 1803-87. He was a prime mover in bringing railways from Knighton to Llandrindod Wells, Presteigne and Radnor. (Perhaps the truck in the previous field would have been a more fitting monument!).*

After the ODP is joined it climbs to another stile, on the edge of a larger wood. From the stile the way lies between conifers on the left and a fence on the right. After a stile in a crossing fence there is a fence on the left and a beautiful view of hills and valleys to the right.

The path is along the top of Offa's Dyke itself, but this is much more obvious after the next stile, where it bends right towards Hawthorn Hill. After another stile and more conifers the ODP bends right with the Dyke, keeping to the right of the summit of the hill. *The Dyke here has the strange characteristic that the ditch is on the east side, the side of Mercia, which would have been completely useless for defending against the Welsh. One wonders whether the local gang of navvies were incompetent or deliberately subversive!*

There is a plantation on the left, succeeded by a fence. After the next stile the fence is on the right, in open pasture where the Dyke almost disappears. After the next stile the ODP turns right and descends with a fence on the right through a small hollow and then over a stile at the bottom of the field. Turn left, now with a fence on the left. Instead of going over the next stile, at an angle of the fence, turn right and head to the right of sheep pens down the field. From there continue with a fence on the left, crossing a small valley. At an angle in the fence turn left through a gate and go down the field on a slight track (of increasing steepness), with a fence and line of hawthorns on the left. The bridleway you are on bears right to meet a more definite track—turn sharp left here through a gate towards Pen-lan [Hilltop] Farm.

Immediately after the gate turn right through a wooden bridle gate down a rough slope with a fence on the right to a similar gate. From this go down the steepening open pasture with a fence on the right to a gate. Go straight down across the next field (towards Whitton) and turn left through a gate from which there is a definite track with a stream down on the right leading to the B4356. Turn right here to return to the start of the walk.

Evenjobb

Interesting scenery, including a fine stretch of Offa's Dyke.

Distance: *4¾ miles, with possible reductions to as little as 3½ miles.*

Start: *In Evenjobb at a three-way junction to the east of the B4357 between Kington and Knighton. There is adequate parking on the wide roads. Grid ref. 265 623 (Landranger 137, Pathfinder 971, Explorer 201).*

By bus: *Sargeant Brothers have a G4 from Llandrindod Wells and New Radnor and a G17 from Knighton and Llangunllo.*

Evenjobb is a small but pleasant village. (The name is pronounced to rhyme with "Devon job".) Lower House (on the right of a piece of land containing a construction of Grecian columns supporting roses) and the house to the right of it are both basically 17th century. There are a Post Office and a church which is about 500 yards north on the B4357. This is actually St Peter's, Evancoyd [Evan's Wood], Evenjobb being the Mercian translation of Evancoyd. It was built at the expense of Mrs Mary Elizabeth Mynors in 1870, when the parish was created. There is information inside the church, but no contents of great interest.

The Route

1. From the three-way junction go up the minor road, past the Post Office. When the road bends right at a large stone barn needing support at one corner fork left. Immediately after passing the last house on the left go left through a waymarked garden gate and go ahead through another similar gate beside a house. Go up a small field to a stile which leads out into a larger field. Keep to the hedge

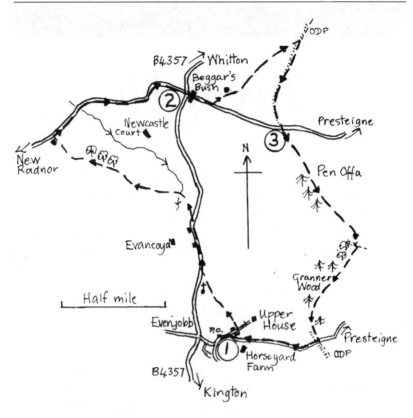

on the right until it bends right and then go across the field, keeping to the right of the churchyard to reach a stile. From this go to the right of a beech tree to the right of a derestriction sign on the B4357, to reach a stile which leads out onto the road.

Turn right along the road, with Home Wood on the left, part of the Evancoyd estate. Pass the drive to the old vicarage (also endowed by Mrs Mynors) on the right. On the left a house (Trappe) is passed, with what appears to be a large walled garden behind it. Also on the left is the drive to Evancoyd (built in 1835) and a lodge, followed soon by a track to "Valley", waymarked as a byway (with red waymarks). This is the route to take unless it is wished to cut out a mile by continuing up the road to Point 2 at the next crossroads in about two thirds of a mile.

On the longer route keep on ahead when the track turns right to a farm, going down to a footbridge beside a ford and then to a wooden gate ahead. The green track climbs from here with deep tractor ruts. Instead of going through a gate ahead bear left on a track which is overshadowed by trees and is rough in places, particularly because of tree roots, and deep below the level of the surrounding fields. (If the track is impassable it may be necessary to use the adjacent fields on the left.)

Eventually the track comes up to field level and there is soon a fine view to the left. *The valley is of the Summergill Brook, with the hills of Radnor Forest (where, according to legend, the last Welsh Dragon still sleeps) to the right. The "pimple" of Whimble appears over the slopes of Stanlo Tump, which are popular for hang-gliding. To the right of the track Newcastle Court, which is partly late Georgian, is down in the valley. Castlering Wood, topped by a small Iron Age Fort, is further round to the right.*

The track is now much more pleasant to walk, and Rhos [Moor] Plantation is soon on the right. Beyond this the track bears right again, in a damper area, and goes ahead when joined by one from the left to pass the farm of Rails Gate and come out onto the B4372. Turn right here and follow the road for nearly a mile. The valley overlooked by Newcastle Court is crossed and there is then a climb past small conifer woods on the right. *To the right the view includes the conical hill of Pen Offa, topped by a plantation and crossed by Offa's Dyke, which will be part of the return route. There may be buzzards mewing and wheeling overhead.* From the crest of the hill the road descends gradually to a crossroads with the B4357.

2. Go ahead onto an unclassified road, with the bluewashed house Northgate (presumably at one time a gatehouse for the Evancoyd estate) on the right and Beggar's Bush Farm on the left. *The lane we are on is part of the ancient route from Radnor Forest to Presteigne.* Pass a track on the right and fork left into a tarmacked track which goes down to Middle House (unless you want to save half a mile - and some climbing - by keeping up the road until it crosses the Offa's Dyke Path at Point 3).

Keep to the right of the farm buildings and go ahead through a metal field gate and down a green enclosed track. This drops down into a valley to cross a trickling stream and then bears left to a gate out into a field. From the gate go across the field to a gate in a fence coming down from the right. Go through this gate and descend slightly in the next field to the nearer of two gates in line. In the next field, as you head to the next gate, the bank of Offa's Dyke can be seen to the right.

Go through the right hand of two gates in the bottom corner and cross the Dyke, which is impressive on either side. *Looking down the line of the Dyke the valley is that of the River Lugg [Bright] and the group of red brick buildings is at Dolley Green, with Hawthorn Hill (see Walk 10) behind.* Turn right, joining the Offa's Dyke Path (ODP) as you do so and climb the field with the Dyke on the right to a stile on the line of the Dyke. The climb continues in the next field with fine oak trees on the Dyke, followed by rowan, hazel and hawthorn.

At the top of the field is another stile on the Dyke and the path continues on the now less impressive Dyke in an open field, with a glorious view to the right to Radnor Forest and the Lugg Valley. Keep on up, ignoring sheep tracks to the right. The next stile is in a hedge coming from the left and the way ahead is now less steep, with a fence and a line of large beeches on the right. At the next stile is one of the fine wooden ODP fingerposts, and then the Dyke and the ODP bend left to a stile and gate before crossing the lane up from Beggar's Bush.

3. From the stile across the lane the hill of Pen Offa [Offa Head] can be seen ahead, with its larch plantation. The path up is between fences, with hawthorns on the left, and the Dyke here is insignificant. Before entering the trees look behind again. *The hill immediately behind now is Llan-fawr [Great Church] and there is a good stretch of the Lugg in sight.* Pen Offa is the highest point on the walk, and it is now effectively downhill all the way. From the stile leading out of the summit area there is another wonderful view ahead. *The nearest wooded ridge is Granner Wood, with Burfa Bank, crowned with another hill fort, behind it and Herrock Hill further back still. Further to the right*

Walking towards Pen Offa

the hillocks in the valley are the wooded Stanner Rocks and Old Radnor Hill, with Hanter Hill behind, connecting to Hergest Ridge.

The path starts down with a mixed conifer wood on the left (giving way to a hawthorn hedge) and a fence on the right. From the stile at the end of the field the path descends steeply to an open area beside a corrugated iron building. Turn left along the track to the top of a small rise. Turn right through an area of bracken and gorse. The ODP soon goes over a stile or through a gate into Granner Wood, which is on the slopes of Evenjobb Hill, the top of which is outside the wood to the left. Through the wood the way is well marked, and is on the line of Offa's Dyke, although this is less obvious than it is elsewhere.

Go down steps into a dip carrying a road. *Walk 12 and the continuation of the ODP are about 10 yards up the road to the left.* To complete this walk leave the ODP by turning right down the road, which is steep and cut through banks. In less than half a mile the road comes down in Evenjobb beside the barn with the supported corner. Turn left to return to the start.

Presteigne

A long but gradual climb through interesting scenery to a fine section of Offa's Dyke. The return is partly on good forestry tracks. (Bring your tree recognition book!)

Distance: *10½ miles. This can be reduced to 10 miles (or even 9) with a lot of road walking, but this would detract from the walk.*

Start: *On the B4355, skirting Presteigne. There are car parks outside the Memorial Hall on the town (north east) side of the road and across the B4355 (which eliminates the need to cross it on foot). Grid ref. 314 642 (Landranger 148, Explorer 201).*

By bus: *Sargeant Brothers run the G5 from Kington and New Radnor.*

Presteigne [Priest-household], once the administrative centre of Radnorshire, is a very pleasant small town, largely unspoiled by "progress". (Incidentally the derivation of "Radnor" is apparently "land of mountain tracks".) There are many fine buildings, including the "Radnorshire Arms" of 1616. This became an inn in 1712, having previously belonged to the Bradshaw family, one of whom was a signatory to the death warrant of King Charles I. There are five other inns, but there were 33 when the London to Aberystwyth stage coaches passed through.

In Broad Street the Judge's Lodging and Courthouse has, as a tourist attraction, been restored to its condition in 1870. Also in the building are the town museum and the TIC. At the bottom of Broad Street is St Andrew's church (which gives rise to the town's Welsh name of Llanandras). It dates in part from Saxon times, includes architecture from then to the 19th century and has some unique contents, including a wooden carillon of 1726 and an early 16th century tapestry.

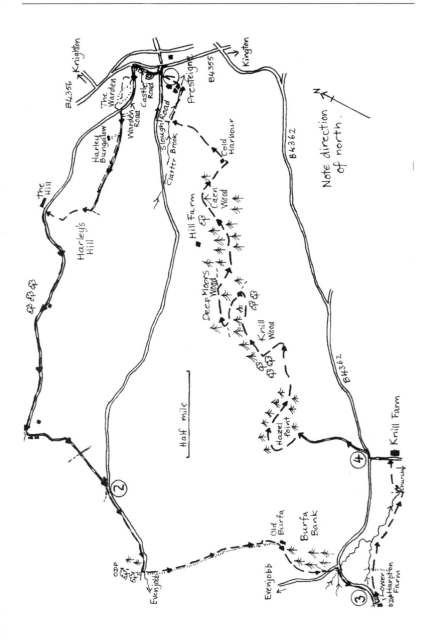

The Route

1. From the car park across the B4355 from the Memorial Hall turn left (north) along the main road, and turn left into Slough Road. For the shortest route Slough Road should be followed for about 2½ miles to Point 2. For the "scenic route" (although this will not be obvious immediately) take the first turn right off Slough Road into Castle Road, and follow this estate road to its end. As Castle Road approaches the B4355 again turn left into Warden Road.

From 1116 until it was levelled by Llewelyn the Last in 1262 Presteigne had a motte and bailey castle on the hillock now known as The Warden, on the right of Warden Road. Now a public park and picnic area, with information boards, it can be investigated and an exit made higher up Warden Road. Be warned, though, that the views are partially masked by trees except during the winter.

If it is wished to visit The Warden turn right at a footpath sign by a stone wall, take the path going uphill to the right and follow a path which curves round and eventually drops down to re-enter Warden Road through a gate. Turn right.

About 50 yards beyond the further entrance to The Warden, turn left on a lane which is also a bridleway. Keep right when a track goes into the field on the left, ascending between tall hedges on a shady lane. When the surfaced track turns right to Harley Bungalow there are two alternatives. You can keep ahead up a green lane, still between hedges, but now with stone and earth underfoot. There are occasional views to the left across the Clatter Brook to the forest through which the walk returns, and also to the right across the valley of the River Lugg (Bright) to the side valley containing the village of Norton. The path goes through a gate and later the hedge on the left is reduced to isolated trees.

The alternative route, which is often drier underfoot, turns along the Harley Bungalow track, but then goes over a stile on the left almost immediately. Go up through three fields, with a stile and then a gate in between, keeping a fence on the left. In the third field go over a stile on the left to rejoin the track just beyond the gate mentioned in the previous paragraph.

Harley's Hill (which will be skirted) is ahead and beautiful quiet country all around. Keep on up the track on the right of the field to a fingerpost at the top. Turn right here on the footpath which keeps level, bearing away from the fence on the right, and passing an isolated sycamore. Turn right over a stile about 20 yards before the gate at the end of the field and go down the field, keeping parallel to the hedge on the left, to another stile which leads back onto the road. *The farm opposite is The Hill, and the valley of the Norton Brook behind it, disappearing into an area of low hills, is pastoral Britain at its best.*

Turn left along the (usually) quiet road, which goes through a gate and winds up the shoulder of Harley's Hill through an open pasture. *The view to the right expands, with the River Lugg coming from the left. (Some of this area is explored in Walk 10 from Whitton.)* There are banks of gorse and bramble on each side of the road as it climbs and then drops down slightly to another gate. After another gate another farm with a modern bungalow farmhouse is passed on a slight ascent, with Gumma [possibly Valleys or Crest] Wood across the field on the right, and the road is again hedged. *As the road bends left the prominent hill ahead is Pen Offa.* The road now descends, gently at first, but then more rapidly into a cluster of houses.

Where there is a junction with a road on the right turn left along a track which soon passes to the left of a farmhouse and farm buildings. The track climbs steadily and winds, with occasional views to the left into the Clatter Brook valley. In season there may be raspberries on the right toward the crest, just before which there is a stile on the right and a green lane on the left. Ignore both and continue on the track which drops down to meet a road, where there is a house on the left. (The road is a continuation of Slough Road.)

2. Go ahead along the road for over half a mile. After a bend to the right, with the road descending quite steeply, there is a wood on the left and a small quarry on the right. After the next bend to the right ignore a track into a Woodlands Trust wood on the right. In about another 150 yards join the Offa's Dyke Path (ODP) by going up steps with a handrail to the left. *(Walk 11 can be joined about 10 yards further down the hill.)*

After climbing up to a stile go left up to the top of the bank of the Dyke, which becomes ever more obvious as it descends. *The view nearby to the right includes the knobble of Old Radnor Hill, with Stanner Rocks being overtopped by Hanter Hill to its left, and Hergest Ridge further to the left. Further away and more to the right are the hills of Radnor Forest.* There is a fence on the left of the ODP except where the ODP switches onto the left of the fence through one field, with the wooded hill of Burfa Bank coming into sight ahead. *This has a fine hillfort on the tap, but it has been much damaged by the afforestation.*

There is another stile with the fence on the left and then another switch across it and back again, with a very deep ditch on the right and a lesser ridge beyond that. The path goes down steeply to cross a ditch and then up again to another stile, where the cross section of the Dyke can be well appreciated.

The ODP drops down to cross a lane, turning left and then, in about 50 yards, right on a roughly surfaced track to pass Old Burfa with its 15th century farmhouse and strongly built barns. Beyond this take the right hand track, which curves round below Burfa Bank, with fields to the right and the steep wooded slope to the left. Keep ahead when a major track comes in from the left and drop down to a road coming from Evenjobb.

Turn left along the road towards a T-junction with the B4362, but before reaching it go over the old Ditchyeld Bridge to the right, crossing the Hindwell and Knobley Brooks. Soon turn right along the B road, with the mass of Herrock Hill (see Walk 13) ahead. The road is rather busy, but is left in about half a mile. Soon after crossing Riddings Brook (and simultaneously going from Powys into Hereford, from Wales into England) Walk 13 is met, coming along past Lower Harpton Farm.

3. Follow the ODP sign in through the gate on the left before the farm and immediately turn left on an unsigned path for which the farmer may have made a way through the crop. The path cuts off corners in the boundary on the left to reach a gate in a fence which is actually on the line of Offa's Dyke. *To the right the Dyke goes up Herrock Hill.* In the next field (a long one) the path runs roughly parallel to the fence on the left, bending right about half way along, to reach a stile in the crossing fence between the edge of the field to the left and a gate to the right. The next field has a parkland feel about it, with scattered clumps of trees, and the path soon joins the fence on the left, with Hindwell Brook behind it.

Level with the second nearby clump of trees in the field there is a new footbridge on the left, which leads across the brook. *It is a wonderful structure and does the job admirably, even if it does appear to be designed to test out three day eventing horses!*

From the footbridge go ahead, with a fence on the right (behind which are the gardens of Tan House). Go through a gateway and bear right to a waymark on a corner of the garden fence. From here go ahead to a gate on the crest of the small ridge (to the left of a large oak tree). From the gateway bear slightly to the left to pass a fence corner and go out through a gate onto a lane.

This is the hamlet of Knill (Knoll) which appeared in Domesday Book as Chenillo, the property of Osborn FitzRichard le Scrob. From about 1242 to early in the 20th century the estate (including Knill Court, which was burnt down in 1942) passed down through the de Kennell, Walsham and Garbett families. The church dates in part from the 12th century. It is heavily restored but contains features of interest, notably a set of nine funeral hatchments, an ancient font and, in the churchyard, most of a 14th century cross. To visit it collect the key from the wonderful Knill Farm (dating from about 1600) across the lane and continue down the lane to the right. When the lane splits bear right over a cattle grid and the church, with its squat tower can soon be seen on a knoll overlooking the stream.

4. To continue the walk, on leaving the field by the gate turn left up the lane to the B4362. Turn right for a short distance to a track on the left. Unless you wish to return to Presteigne along the road turn left up the track, which is labelled as a Public Byway. In about half a mile the track reaches a wood, with the hillock of Hazel Point ahead. There are many tracks through the wood, so please be careful to keep to the recommended route!

Go over the stile beside the Forestry Commission gate and turn left along the main track which climbs and bends round to the right, with a field outside the wood to the left. Go through an open area and continue on the main track. Ignore lesser paths and a crossing track as you climb through a deciduous part of the wood with beech and oak prominent. Another grassy track goes off to the right, with the higher ground to the left, and a slope down to the right. The track continues to climb, with a steep slope down on the right and then comes out to where there is an open view across a valley in front.

This is part of Knill Wood, and the track bears left to skirt round the valley head, levelling off. Again there is a grassy track going left as the main track continues through beeches. At a major three way junction turn left. *(You have now returned into Powys.)* The well surfaced track is level at first and bends round to the left. Pass a grassy track on the left and then do a slow U-turn to the right and descend. *This is now Deep Moors Wood.* Ignore another good grassy track on the left and climb a little. It should be possible to glimpse Hill Farm down below across the valley between the trees on the left.

The track is basically level, with just minor ups and downs and then there is a more sustained gentle climb into Caen Wood. After levelling off the track bends to the right and goes definitely down with views over to the left towards Presteigne. Leave the track at last to pass immediately in front of a house on the left [Cold Harbour]. Pass the house and turn left to go through a (previously hidden) gate on the left. From here go down the field with a fence on the left, through a gateway and down the next field, again with a fence on the left.

Bear right going down the next field to a projecting field corner from which the way is again down with a fence on the left. Go through a gate to a bank above the Clatter Brook. If the brook is carrying much water go ahead over the bridge and bear slightly left to a stile onto Slough Road, where you should turn right.

If the brook is low turn right along the bank before the bridge. Stepping stones lead across the stream and soon back again and the path then continues with the stream on the left and new housing beyond it. Cross the stream on a bridge and go along the facing track. This leads to Slough Road, where you should turn right and right again to return to the starting point. (Note that the imaginatively decorated underpass at the end of Slough Road leads directly to the centre of the town, not to the Memorial Hall.)

Knill Church

Kington and Herrock Hill

The outward walk is gentle except for possibly overgrown sections. The return climbs over Herrock and Rushock Hills, with excellent views and sections of the Dyke.

Distance: *8 miles, which can be walked in two sections, of 5¾ and 2½ miles.*

Start: *Start in The Square, Kington, which is off Church Street. There is parking in The Square and just beyond it. Grid ref. 296 567 (Landranger 148, Pathfinder 971 - 933 also needed, Explorer 201). If the smaller loop is walked separately park near Lower Harpton Farm, grid ref. 278 603 on Landranger 148, Explorer 201, and start the walk from point 3.*

By bus: *Kington is accessible by bus from from Presteigne (service G5) and from Hereford and Llandrindod Wells (services 461 & 462). All these services are run by Sargeant Brothers and pass through New Radnor. All services run to the car park in Mill Street, near the bottom of Church Street. Lower Harpton (or Hopton) is served by the very early G5 from Kington (again Sargeant Brothers).*

Kington is well worth exploring, with many interesting buildings, and the advantage of "real" shops which do not have to compete with large supermarkets. The TIC on Mill Street, near the interesting little museum, has information about the town and its history, which dates back to 1052. In Domesday Book it was spelt "Chingtune", apparently Old English for "Royal Manor" or "Royal Town". The church, with its steeple looking rather like a pile of three traffic cones, dates in parts from about 1200. In spite of the usual Victorian restoration there is much of interest including a Norman font and, outside, the base of a medieval preaching cross.

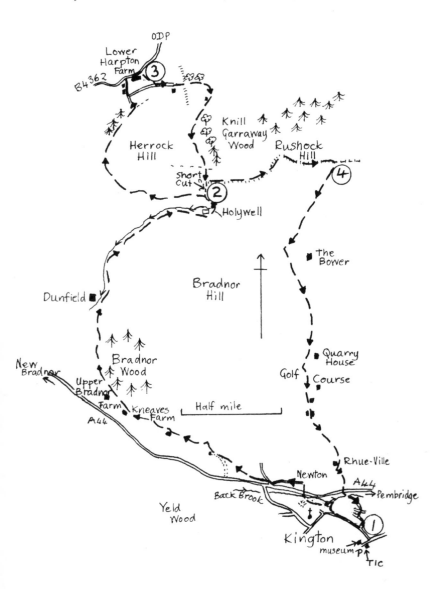

The Route

1. From the end of The Square, which has an 18th century terrace next to a 17th century house, go up Church Street, passing between the Swan (on the right) and the Royal Oak (on the left). *Kington is well supplied with public houses, but not the full 31 inns which it has had. The Royal Oak is the only one which still has a mounting block.* Pass Doctors Lane, a small road on the right, and continue up, with walls on either side. Immediately before a whitewashed house turn right on a waymarked footpath through a metal kissing gate and go down the walled path overhung with trees. The path bears right, with a metal fence on the left.

On reaching the valley bottom turn sharply left through another metal kissing gate on a path below the one down from the town, on what was once a railway line. *There is a paddock on the right, with the Back Brook and the A44 road beyond it. Above to the left is Castle Hill,*

The Square, Kington

where a castle (probably wooden) stood in the 12th century. Part way along a stretch beside the brook, which has a pleasant waterslide, is another kissing gate.

Turn right to cross the brook by a metal and concrete bridge and then cross the A44 with care.

Glance back at Castle Hill and then climb a flight of wooden steps. Turn left at the top down a lane above rooftops to the left. *This is the district of Newton.* The lane drops down to the A44 again, now in Floodgates, but instead of turning left to the main road go ahead along the tarmacked track parallel to it. *The nearby Floodgates Bridge was demolished in a great storm in 1795 and reconstructed only in 1811.*

When the track comes to an end at a turning circle go through a gate on the right and follow the direction of the footpath waymark, slanting up across the field to a gateway to the right of a stone and wood barn with a corrugated iron roof. Continue straight ahead in the next field to a stile slightly to the right of a large tree and keep the same direction to join a track with grass between the tarmac strips, which comes up from the road towards a house.

To the left Yeld Wood covers the lower slopes of Hergest Ridge across the valley. Before the brick gateposts, turn back right through a gate into a field and then turn left to go up the slope to the right of a fence on the left of the field. Keep close to the fence and go over two stiles in quick succession. Keep to the left of the fence ahead, losing as little height as possible, with a good view along the Back Brook valley to the left.

Keep to the right of hawthorn trees ahead to come out onto a tarmac track just beyond a cattle grid. Continue in the same direction along the track, soon with a conifer plantation on the right. Follow the track round a bend to the left and then turn right before a house beside the track.

Go through a metal gate onto a clear track which goes along near the bottom of Bradnor Wood. Before the next metal gate fork right through a wooden gate. Climb slightly between beech trees and turn left down a forest ride which may be brambly. Keep near the fence on the left hand edge of the wood above Kneaves Farm to the left and beyond to where Upper Bradnor Farm is on the left. At the end of a field on the left the track goes ahead through another plantation of conifers and bears right. As the track bends back sharply to the left go right through a gate into a field.

Go across this on the level to the left of a power line pole. *The bracken covered slopes of Bradnor Hill can be seen to the right up the shallow valley and to the left the Gilwern Brook comes between the wooded slopes of Worsell Wood to the left and Stanner Rocks to the right.* Beyond the pole a gate is reached with a stile beside it. From this go ahead with a fence on the left with rhododendrons beyond it, and bracken and open woodland to the right. *The large farm which can be glimpsed to the left is Dunfield.* Beyond the farm take a stile on the left and keep on the level in the next field, joining a stony track from the farm. Follow this through a metal gate and then through the next field, with a trickling stream to the left and Herrock Hill in front.

The track bends right to a gate with a waymark. Follow it through the gate and the next two fields as it gradually bends right towards the valley head, eventually climbing more obviously. Cross the stream near the ruins of Holywell, which was a 17th century timber-framed cottage. Beyond the ruins bear left to a waymarked stile in the fence, from which you should go across the field to a waymarked gate, as you start to go down the other side of the little valley. Go through the gate.

2. If you wish to take a short cut turn right up through the bracken to reach the Offa's Dyke Path on Herrock Hill at the top of the slope, shortly before Point 4. To continue with the full (and very scenic) walk go ahead with a hedge of hazel, blackthorn and hawthorn (and the occasional rose) on the left. The path is now skirting Herrock Hill and is very easy to follow, with a hedge or fence on the left. Ignore any paths going to the left.

As the path bends to the right, Navages Wood is over to the left, across fields. The hills which come into sight to the left later are those of Radnor Forest, going up to over 2000 feet, and to the right of them the spire of the church at Evenjobb (see Walk 11) should be visible. After this views to the left are cut off by a band of spruce, with a few deciduous trees, but the isolated hill of Burfa Bank comes into sight ahead.

Burfa Bank is topped by an Iron Age fort, probably built by the Decangi. The afforestation has prevented a through investigation of the complex site of this, but it probably has a complicated barbican entrance on the south.

The path now descends towards Lower Harpton Farm. Go through a metal gate ahead into an enclosed track, soon joining a better track which comes from the right. There are two houses on the left of the track before it comes out onto a road (the B4362). Turn right here and pass the entrance to Lower Harpton Farm.

3. *At the end of the farm the walk links with Walk 13, which comes along the road to the left, and also joins the Offa's Dyke Path (ODP).* Immediately beyond the farm buildings turn right through a gate or over a stile and pass the side of the farm buildings. Go ahead to another gate and stile and then bear left to a gate in a crossing hedge, which leads out into a hedged track. *As you look to the left before the gate the hedgeline in the field is on Offa's Dyke, and this will soon be crossed as it goes steeply up Herrock Hill.*

Go left along the track, passing below a cottage, and continue past stored machinery to go through or over a gate or stile, still on a good track, which is now climbing steadily, with a fence on the left and bracken covered slopes to the right. Keep to the track, which goes to the right of a facing gate which leads into the wood, and soon negotiate another gate or stile. Keep to the left of a small barn with a gated enclosure in front of it and fork right where indicated, to climb amongst bracken and scattered trees. *On the climb the view to the left is along the valley of Hindwell Brook.*

When a fence coming from the right is met there are another gate and stile, after which the fence is on the left. Keep on up and ahead on the obvious path when the fence turns left. *Looking back now the top of Burfa Bank can be seen and there appear to be visible traces of the earthworks of the fort.* Knill Garroway Wood, with fine conifers, is close on the left as the path climbs and the path bends right (as indicated) past a small hawthorn. On the crest a path crosses the ODP and on a clear day it is well worth turning right on it to the summit of Herrock Hill, which gives wonderful views.

Soon the ODP turns left at another crossing path. (The path ahead here is the short cut from Point 2 near Holywell.) The ODP now follows Offa's Dyke itself, often covered in bracken, up towards the summit of Rushock [Rushy place or reed-bed] Hill, with another gate and stile on the way. Shortly before the top the Dyke is crossed at a point where it is more obvious and the path then goes along the top of the Dyke with a fence on the left, and much of the outward route in view behind to the right. From a stile the finest stretch of the Dyke on this walk goes on ahead, with the ODP just to its left, to reach the summit of Rushock Hill.

At 1245 feet this is the highest point of the walk (even though it is not quite "downhill all the way" from here on). There are views ahead to the east over Herefordshire as well as the ones to west and south that we have been seeing before. Only to the north is there no view, because of a spur of Knill Garroway Wood. The Dyke and the ODP turn right here, descending to another stile where they bend left, the Dyke being particularly clear.

4. Before the next stile the ODP and this walk turn right, but Offa's Dyke goes ahead, accompanied by the Mortimer Trail, which runs for 30 miles between Kington and Ludlow. *(The Dyke is not seen on any of the later walks in this book.)* Bradnor [Broad, flat-topped Ridge] Hill is now ahead, the slopes on this side being much gentler than those above the outward route. The ODP descends to a hedge corner, where the way is ahead through a gate or over a stile and then has a fence on the left. On the descent into a small valley the fence bears away to the left but the ODP continues ahead towards a fence coming down off Bradnor Hill.

Again there is a choice of gate or stile, from which the path bears left, a fingerpost to the right of the gate giving the direction. Go over a stile, down into a valley and then climb to a stile in a post and wire fence. *The farm across to the left is The Bower.* From here it is half right to a stile in another fence. Next head to a fence corner in front of a clump of trees and then bear right, keeping the oak plantation on the left. After another gate and stile the path bears away from the wood to a fence on the right which is followed to the next gate, level with Quarry House with its bright red roofs. After going through the gate a lane is reached along which the ODP goes, to enter the National Trust property of Bradnor Hill and a golf course, (where more waymarks would be useful).

The ODP crosses a tarmac track and then goes half left, to the right of the first green post and down a shallow depression (pointing towards Kington church) crossing two fairways. Then go ahead on a track through the bracken, with a little old quarry to the right. Cross another track and keep to the right of a whitewashed cottage, to descend a slope (now with better waymarking) to more white houses. Cross another track and go down to the left of a house beside it. *This area is Bradnor Green.*

A little way down the track go through a painted gate onto an enclosed path between houses, which leads to a kissing gate. The path leads into an open field and goes down to two gates (kissing and field), beside a beech tree. *On the way down Kington is ahead looking surprisingly extensive.*

From the gates the path is enclosed between hedges, coming down beside Rhue-Ville Farm, and then goes across a small field to a gate which leads onto the farm road. Turn left along this and descend to the A44 again. Cross with care again to a wooden bridge which leads back over Back Brook to a street (Crooked Well) lined with picturesque old cottages. *(Crooked Well was once Kington's only source of water.)* Turn left along the road, which turns to the right and climbs. Keep on ahead with estate roads to left and right. At the top turn left into a car park and then right into The Square.

The car park was the site for Kington's fairs, which date back to 1265 and at one time, took place eight times per year.

Gladestry

A pleasant, pastoral walk, the three options giving successively greater climbs and consequently better views of Hanter Hill and the Hergest Ridge and beyond.

Distance: *4½, 5½ or 6 miles.*

Start: *Begin in Gladestry, which is on the B4594 about 4 miles west of Kington. There is a parking area opposite the PO and store, beside the Royal Oak public house. (There is also a good layby on the B4594 just north of the village.) Grid ref. 233 552 (Landranger 148, Pathfinder 993, Explorer 201).*

By bus: *Apart from school buses the only service to Gladestry is the 464 from Kington which runs on Tuesdays only. Both it and the School buses are run by Sargeant Brothers.*

Gladestry [Open space or clearing] (pronounced almost to rhyme with "pastry") is only small, but has a number of old buildings. The fabric of the church dates from the 13th to 15th centuries, but was restored in 1910. Inside there are many features of interest, and the outside includes the tower which was built in sections from the base in the 15th century to the spire in 1709, and an unusual Sanctus bellcote at the junction of nave and chancel roofs. Behind the church is a medieval tithe barn, with the typical local ventilation slits, the effect being spoilt by a corrugated iron roof.

The Route

1. From the road junction at the east end of the village follow the sign to Newchurch, walking along the footway on the left, past the Royal Oak and Gladestry Court, which has a date of 1689 near the chimney breast. Keep left with the main road where a road goes right past the church, with a 16th century black and white cottage on the corner.

Cross over the Gladestry Brook and turn left immediately into a lane, with an Offa's Dyke Path (ODP) acorn waymark. *The high hedges either side are thick with flowers in season and have a variety of trees in them, including some vast ash trees. The lane itself, unusually, has storm drains down the centre.* Almost imperceptibly the lane crosses a stream (the Wernol [Swallow] Brook) where there is a track on the right to Burnt House and the lane then starts to climb. At the top of the rise the farm on the right is the 18th century Stone House - from the wood piled in the yard "Wood House" might seem more apt, but the name may derive from the old quarry beyond the farm.

As the lane bears right beyond the farm, take a waymarked stile on the right. The path climbs gently through a meadow and then up a short steeper slope out of the old quarry area. Turn left at the top of the steep slope and climb more gently, with the quarry on the left and slightly higher ground on the right. A waymark shows the way past a more obvious small quarry on the right. *Behind, the Hergest Ridge has the almost detached Hanter Hill on its left and Old Radnor Hill further back.*

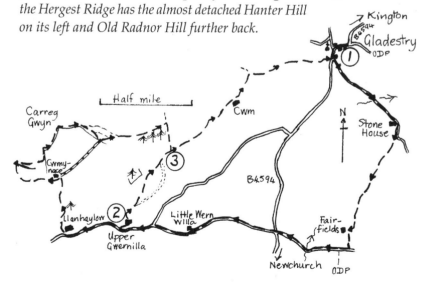

Continue to climb gently in the same direction, now on a stony track. At the top of the rise go over two stiles in quick succession (or through the accompanying gates) and then turn left to continue the climb, with a hawthorn hedge on the left. After the next stile and gate, at the top of the next small rise, turn right, with a wire fence on the right and descend towards what was Stonehouse Barn. *This seems to have been recently turned into an elegant dwelling, now named Fairfields, with newly laid out gardens.* Turn left over a stile before the garden and go along an enclosed path beside it. *Some of the unusual trees on the right are eucalyptus, but (so far at any rate) there are no koalas or 'possums in sight!* At the end of the path come out onto a road and turn right, linking with Walk 15.

The ODP turns left over a stile very soon, but this walk continues along the road, which descends gently to cross the Wernol Brook again and then climbs rather more steeply. Go across the crossroads with the B4594 (unless the road to the right is required for a quick return to Gladestry). The lane ahead is signposted to Colva [Low Peak] and Glascwm [Green Valley]. At first the lane climbs gently. *At the top of the hill there is a fine view to the right along the valley of the Gladestry Brook.* The road descends past Little Wern Willa and then into a wooded valley, passing a small wood which is on the right. Turn left at a T-junction with a major road. After crossing another stream climb slightly, passing below a farm [Upper Gwernilla] on the right, to the farm drive.

2. From here there are two ways. The shorter turns back right along the drive to the farm. Go between the main farm buildings and turn left at a facing one. Go through three gates (which may or may not be closed) and go down the facing track. Before a crossing wooden fence turn right along a more obvious track, which descends into the tree-filled valley bottom. After crossing the stream go ahead through a gate and in about 30 yards the right of way turns left through another gate into a field (although the farmer might prefer you to keep to the track, which goes into the next field and then climbs to rejoin the right of way shortly before point 3). On the official route head up the field, aiming beyond the right hand corner of the wood at the top. Go through a gateway just beyond the wood and turn right, with the remains of a hawthorn and hazel hedge on the right. At the end of the field go through a gate and go ahead, now with a hedge on the left. Go through another facing gate, and again go ahead, rejoining the longer routes at point 3.

For the longer routes continue along the road from Upper Gwernilla for nearly half a mile to the next farm on the right (Llanhaylow). Turn right along the tarmac track on the left of the farm buildings. Go through a gate and continue on the track as it curves down to the right. The track winds through the valley bottom, crossing the stream and passing through another gate, and then climbs to the buildings of Cwm-y-nace. The middle route turns right here along the enclosed track, to rejoin the longest route (which goes through some thick bracken) when it emerges onto an open moor.

The official right of way behind Cwm-y-nace is impracticable, but passing in front of the farm three gates in succession lead into a pasture. Head for the gate straight ahead, in a wood and wire fence, and from this head for the bottom of the steep slope slightly to the right. Keep to the left of a clump of ash trees and then bear round to the right on a grassy shelf which slopes upward to a gate.

Go through the gate and in about ten yards branch back right on a path which initially runs with a fence on the right, and then branches up left through the bracken about 90 yards before a tree by the fence. The path climbs fairly steadily between hawthorns. (But for the bracken it would be a good path and appears to have been well used at one time.) The last hawthorn bush is on the path, which then becomes less clear, but soon a post and wire fence coming up from near Cwm-y-nace is met. Turn left up the fence following it round to the right shortly after a fence junction on the right. Ignore a gate on the right and pass a number of hawthorns. At the next fence corner bear right again, joining a more definite track.

The hill to the left is Carreg Gwyn [White Stone] an outlier of Cefn-hir [Longback]. On the descent the view that you have come up here to see gradually unfolds in front of you, and I hope that it is worth the climb. The most obvious features are the mass of Hergest Ridge, with Hanter

Hill tacked onto its left, and the valley of Gilwern [Recess of marsh or alders] Brook below. Old Radnor Hill is across the valley from Hanter Hill and Herrock Hill (see Walk 13) may be seen between them.

On two occasions when the track splits take the right fork, to meet the track from Cwm-y-nace, which comes through a gate on the right. Turn left through the gap in the bracken and then bear slightly left to join the other tracks from the left, always aiming towards the right end of a row of pine trees. The track bears left through a gate and then right above a belt of cypress, with the view to the left over the plain becoming more extensive. The track, now stony, descends quite steeply. Once past all the trees turn right at a T-junction of tracks (the main one going left to a farm). Through a gate the grassy track descends between fences. At another track T-junction (where that on the right is from Upper Gwernilla) turn left.

3. Keep close to the fence and hedgerow on the right, with Old Radnor and Hanter Hills ahead. Leave the field by a gate ahead (ignoring another gate to the right) and continue down the next field on the left of a fenced-off ditch, turning right with its fence. Go towards a gate ahead, but turn left before it to descend more steeply on a more obvious track, with a fence and hedgerow on the right. Pass through a gate and keep to the left of the farm buildings of Cwm [Valley]. Continue down an enclosed track between flowery hedges and turn right at a crossing track, on a less used track, away from the buildings of Newhouse Farm.

A metal gate leads into a field. Turn left, with the hedge on the left, still on a slight track, and cross a stream on a footbridge. Continue in the same direction, now with the stream on the left, to go through a gateway. Follow the track, which curves away from the stream, and go through another gate in a crossing hedge. Keep across the next field, descending slightly, to reach a gate in the corner with the left hand hedge. Having gone through this keep close to the left hand hedge, bearing right part way along to reach a gate onto the B4594, opposite where it was left on the outward route. Turn left and bear right to return to the starting point.

Huntington and Newchurch

The village of Huntington, has a lovely old church and castle ruins. The outward journey to Newchurch includes an exhilarating stretch over Disgwylfa Hill; the return is through very pleasant rural scenery.

Distance: *7½ miles.*

Start: *Start in Huntington, which is about 5 miles southwest of Kington. It is possible to park where the road goes down towards the church (grid ref. 249 536). There is also a car park at the village hall (grid ref. 248 537. Landranger 148, Pathfinder 993, Explorer 201).*

By bus: *The only possible bus is the 464 from Kington on Tuesdays only (Sargeant Brothers). (Note that at the time of writing this allows a "window" of less than four hours for the walk.)*

In the 13th century it was planned that what is now the quiet hamlet of Huntington would replace Kington as the most important township in the area, but Kington's position was so well established that this did not happen. Huntington has its own lengthy history, though. A pre-Norman castle associated with Earl Harald Hardrada was superseded by a Norman one, probably built by a de Bohun about 1250. In 1264 Prince Edward, later to become Edward I, besieged and captured it. Some traces remain.

The church, one of few whose dedication to St Thomas a Becket was not withdrawn in Henry VIII's time, has many features of interest, although restored from dilapidation only in 1890. The walls (one of the 13th century) are all massive, as are many of the pews. Otherwise Huntington has few facilities nowadays—a Post Office and The Swan public house, which is apparently open only in the evening.

The Route

1. Start where the west end of the loop road which goes past the pub and towards the church leaves the "back road" between Kington and Newchurch. (Grid ref. 248 537) *It is possible to explore the remains of the Norman castle on the nearby knoll, but much of it is overgrown, and there is only one significant piece of masonry standing.* Set off along the lane opposite the road to the village, to the right of the new village hall, and follow this as it bears round to the left, over a cattle grid, in an open field as a tarmac track. Cross over a second cattle grid and go ahead through the farmyard of Llanerch-y-frain [Crow Glade], ignoring bridleways on each side.

Newchurch parish church

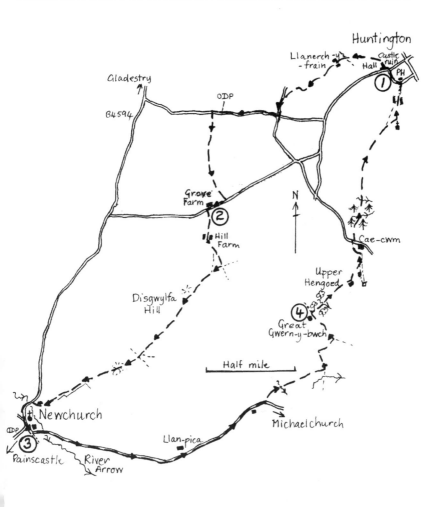

Go on through a green-painted gate between two buildings faced in corrugated iron, ignore gates to right and left and take one which leads into an enclosed track which climbs and then levels off. The track bends right and then left and reaches a lane. Turn left here and soon right on the major road at a crossroads. The road climbs at first and then goes down slightly. The Offa's Dyke Path (ODP) sign on the right is part of Walk 14. Take the ODP sign in about 50 yards on the left, just before the elegant drive on the right to Fairfields.

The stile leads to an uncomfortably narrow path on the right of a long field. At the end of this there is a stile from which the path climbs and bends slightly left towards a plantation on a hill. After another stile keep on with a fence on the right to a stile and gate onto a road. Turn right here and pass Grove Farm.

2. Turn left down a well-surfaced track and through a gate to Hill Farm. Keep straight on between the farmhouse on the left and the farm buildings on the right onto a stony track which bears left with hedges on each side. A gate leads onto a common, which is the start of the fine path over Disgwylfa [Watchtower or Meeting Place] Hill. *(This might sound like a likely place for a Jehovah's Witnesses convention, but there probably aren't enough doorsteps.)* Keep left at the first fork to reach a fingerpost which indicates a sharp right turn. The track climbs between bracken to climb over the first summit of Disgwylfa Hill. *The valley of the River Arrow is down to the left, with Michaelchurch-on-Arrow beyond it. Further on, the Wye Valley near Hay should be seen on a clear day.*

The path skirts to the left of the summit and you should then take the right fork again before dropping down into the possibly damp depression between the two summits. There are occasional waymarks, but basically it is straight on here and up over the second, slightly lower summit. *All is now grass rather than bracken and the area is much used by horse riders. On the descent the upper part of the Arrow valley is seen to the right, and the church at Newchurch can be seen ahead, in line with the road going on towards Painscastle.*

The downward slope is gradual to start with but increases. Keep to the right of a fence corner and continue down with the fence on the left, again keeping outside the fence at another protruding corner. Keep close to the fence and then enter an enclosed track through a gate. The track descends rapidly, turns right, crosses a stream and goes in front of a farmhouse to reach the B4594. Turn left along this, crossing the River Arrow into Newchurch. Go up the footway on the right of the road, passing a chapel, to a crossroads.

Newchurch (the latest church is Victorian, but the site dates back to Saxon times) has little by way of facilities—no pub, no shop and no bus service—in spite of being on a Roman road. A visit to the church is enlivened by typewritten quotations and items of interest, which are scattered around. It was visited by the Rev Francis Kilvert, writer of the famous "Diaries" (see Introduction), who often walked over from Clyro to visit the vicar and his family. On one such occasion two of the vicar's young daughters were assisting with castrating lambs! The church font is 10th or 11th century. Behind the church The Great House (not open) apparently has the widest cruck hall in: Wales, dating from 1490.

3. Leave Newchurch along the road beside the church, with a signpost to Michaelchurch, and keep to the road for about 1¼ miles. Alongside the Great House, take a left fork rather than going along the lane which is the route for the ODP, and soon cross the River Arrow. *This will accompany us on the right as it meanders along its valley—obviously not the arrow with a reputation for straightness! Disgwylfa Hill rises to the left. At the right time of year there are plenty of flowers to admire.* The road gradually climbs up from the valley bottom, passes Llan-pica [Pointed Church] Farm and then descends again. There is a bungalow, Glen-haven, on the right. When the road bends right shortly after this take the track to the left.

Go in through the field gate ahead, not the one on the left, and proceed with a fence on the left. *(The right of way should strictly be along the blocked fenced track on the left.)* Go through a gate in the next fence and turn left to go through another gate. Turn right to proceed in the original direction, now with the fence on the right. Cross a stream and continue ahead on a track which bends to the right. Go through a gate and continue with a fence on the right, now in open pasture. At the end of the field go through a gate and head towards another slightly to the right, not towards a footbridge over the Arrow further to the right.

Having gone through the gate turn left and climb the hill with a fence on the left. At a well-laid blackthorn and elder hedge turn right and go with it on the left. *To the right, across the valley, the church of Michaelchurch-on-Arrow (more accurately above-Arrow) can be seen. Milton Hill is some distance to the right of the church.* Go through a gate in the wire fence ahead and continue round left into the corner of the field, where a waymarked gate gives access to a lane. The lane climbs to pass Great Gwern-y-bwch [Buck Meadow].

4. Immediately after passing the farm go through a field gate on the right and cross the field to a corner of the wood opposite. From the corner go for a few yards with the wood on the left and then turn into the wood. Cross a trickle of a stream and then turn right to cross a brook by a plank bridge. Immediately, go over a waymarked stile and go slightly to the right to climb the slope to a waymarked tree stump, where you leave the wood. Head for a gate ahead, almost in line with a hillock. Through the gate proceed with a fence on the right to a stile in the fence, just over the crest of the hill. Go over the stile and turn left to a gateway in line with the farm ahead (Upper Hengoed [Old Wood]).

Go ahead to and through the gate into the farmyard. Keep to the left of all the buildings, passing through another gate, to a stile on the left before a building which blocks the way. The stile is soon followed by a garden gate, which leads out into a field. Head to the right, aiming for a stile about half way along the wooden fence to the left of a wooden barn and then head into the far right corner of the field, to a stile onto the farm track. *The tree-crowned hummock back to the right, known as Turret Tump, is an old motte.*

Having left the field in the corner go through the gate on the left and then over the stile on the left, to follow a waymarked path which goes across a field full of farm machinery to a gate and then goes to the right up to a stile on the skyline. From this go right, down to a gate onto a road. (If bus users are running short of time they can get onto the bus route before Huntington by turning left here and following signs to Huntington.) Turn right for a few yards, left into a yard and then onto a footpath on the right of a barn. At the end of this a stile leads out near a duck pond. Keep to the left of this, go through a gate and up the right of the field to a wooden gate, soon followed by a metal one. Continue as indicated by the waymarks, with the hedge on the right.

Unless extra waymarks have been put in it is advisable to keep to this hedge until the track is about to enter the wood and then turn left with a fence still on the right in order to reach a wooden footbridge over a stream. Climb up into a field and, once you can see it, bear rightish down into a grassy hollow, where there is a waymarked gate. *On the way down the hill of Hergest Ridge is prominent ahead.* Before the gate cross over a trickling stream and after it head up the field to another gate. Go through the left of two gates and continue, with a fence on the right. At the end of the field go through a gateway and through the next field on a stony track, with woodland at the edge of the field to the right.

Go over a cattle grid into the next field and continue on the track to an ash tree in mid-field. If you wish to visit the church (much recommended if you have time) bear right with the track, otherwise go ahead into the corner of the field. In either case pass between the buildings of Upper House Farm on the obvious route, pass the Post Office and reach the road near The Swan. Turn left and go round a right hand bend to reach the starting point.

St Thomas a Becket church, Huntington

Rhydspence and Pentwyn

This is a fine walk with beautiful views of the Wye valley, interesting landscapes and an old chapel, but some of the footpaths can be overgrown, so it may be advisable to have a stick to beat down nettles etc.

Distance: *7¼ miles, with an extra ¼ mile to visit the chapel at Bettws Clyro or 5½ miles with a short cut.*

Start: *Rhydspence is on the A438, approximately NNE of Hay-on-Wye. Parking is probably available in the Rhydspence Inn's car park, if permission is requested. Otherwise the loop off the A438 through Rhydspence is reasonably wide. Grid ref. 242 473 (Landranger 148, Pathfinder 1016, Explorer 201).*

By bus: *The only service to Rhydspence is the 445 from Llandrindod Wells, Builth Wells and Hay-on-Wye, run on Wednesdays and Saturdays by Roy Browns Coaches.*

Rhydspence [Rhyd = ford] is little more than a scatter of houses and the picturesque, 16th century Rhydspence Inn, which may have originated as a drovers' inn - a far cry from its present status. In 1872 the Reverend Francis Kilvert (see Introduction), after heavy flooding, described it as having four inches of mud inside.

The Route

1. Start as though coming out of the inn and turn right onto the loop road. Take the lane slanting up to the left off the loop road. The lane

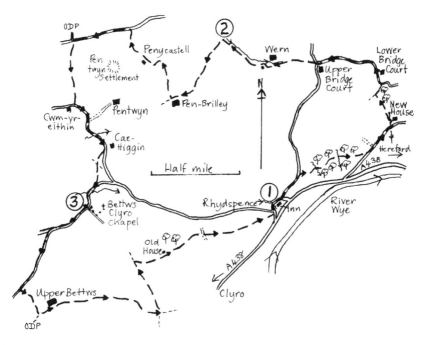

is narrow, with hedges on each side. Pass a house on the right and continue steeply up into a wood, passing several white-painted gates on the right. Just after a large spreading oak tree and before reflector posts on the right go up to a stile on the right. This leads to a bridge across a ditch, and the path goes to the left into a meadow with grassed-over humps. Keep to the right of the meadow for about 40 yards and then go under a branch with a waymark on it. Cross a trickle of a stream and go right between trees for a few yards onto a better path. Turn left along this into a second tussocky open space. Go along to the far end of this and go left over a waymarked stile.

Over this drop down through a wood (Rhydspence Plantation) to a stream, which is crossed on large stones. After crossing the stream bear right to take a path slanting up gently to the right, through tall trees, many of them coppiced. The path bends left, crosses a trickle of a stream, which it goes beside until nearly at the edge of the wood. Bear right here, as indicated, ignoring the path to the left. A clear path now descends, crossing a trickle and then a culverted stream and bends to the right. Bend left and descend with an open space on the left. Now on a track pass through an open area which slants to the right, with a house on the left which must have a fine view of the Wye below to the right. *Merbach [Little Marrow] Hill is across it to the left.*

The track continues below a large sweet chestnut tree to a stile and gate which lead out onto a road by a post box. Turn left along the road, which climbs gradually with occasional glimpses of the Wye and the A438 below to the right. Pass a track to the left and the entrance to a bungalow to the right. When the road bends right follow a footpath sign on the left, which initially leads up a tarmacked track to New House. *(Which is something of a misnomer now.)*

Pass to the left of the house and turn left over a stream on the first small bridge. Keep the hedge on the left as you climb on a path which may be somewhat overgrown, to reach a double stile, the second part being over an electric fence insulated with a rubber sleeve. From this keep up the meadow, keeping close to the hedge on the left. *Soon there is a good view to the left along the Wye valley, with Hay Bluff prominent across the valley.*

(If the path from the bridge is impassable it may be necessary to walk up the meadow, go through a gate and rejoin the path on the left at the top of the next meadow just before the belt of woodland referred to in the next paragraph.)

There may be another electrified fence to be crossed before the hedge at the top of the field is reached. There are another insulated section of electrified fence and a stile adjacent to the hedge on the left to be crossed before you can go through a small belt of traditional woodland to enter an area which is planted with spruce. Keep to the left up through this, with a variety of small flowers, including scarlet pimpernel. Turn right at a crossing fence and keep on the track which has developed to a gate on the left which leads out onto a tarmacked lane.

Turn left along the lane, soon passing Lower Bridge Court, a pleasant, partly black-and-white half-timbered house on the right. *(It dates from the 14th or 15th century.)* The lane bends left and climbs between hedges which include honeysuckle and foxglove. Eventually the lane comes to a crossing road at a grass triangle, with Upper Bridge Court on the left. The way ahead is through the right hand of a pair of gates, as indicated by a waymark (or over the adjacent stile). The right of way goes diagonally across the field, towards some corrugated iron roofs, but these are out of sight in mid-field.

To leave the field climb a waymarked stile and bear left along the hawthorn and elder hedge. When the hedge bears left, bear right towards the middle of the open barn at Wern [Alder Trees] Farm to reach a gate which leads into the yard. Turn right as indicated, keeping the barn on the left and turn left just before the stream into a trackway with trees on each side. It may be necessary to unfasten a hurdle to proceed along the track, which soon comes out into an open field by a gate or stile. Continue with a fence on the right, with a stream behind it, climbing gently up a large field. At the top of the field go over a stile and turn left.

2. Climb with a wire fence on the left and a hedge on the right. Keep close to the fence on the left, with the path becoming enclosed and then the trees on the right becoming sporadic. A pair of stiles, before and after a gate on the right, are met and are climbed to get into the next field. Keep near the fence on the right in this narrow field, passing under a large hornbeam tree. At the crest of the hill pass into the next field in which you descend with a winding hedge on the right. *(To the left is a wonderful panorama.)* Pass under two large oaks and a sycamore, after which a stile down on the right is taken. Keep to the left of the hedge, which bends round to the right of Pen-Brilley [Top woodland clearing where broom grows], with a stile as the farm is approached.

Keep to the right of the buildings and turn right on a stony track which goes over a cattle grid and climbs again to a little crest and then descends gradually. The track bends left and right and passes to the right of the buildings of Pen-y-castell [Castle Head], which are in various states of disrepair. *The castle in question is the early hill fort of Pentwyn (Hillhead) on the hill behind, round three sides of which we will now walk. It was built by the Decangi and is small—less than two acres.* The track climbs, winds and descends before going over a cattle grid to come out onto a road.

Turn left along the road. *From this direction Pentwyn is behind a conifer plantation. The verges are mainly bracken, but there are dog roses in the hedgerows, and, in the summer and autumn, plenty of burdocks, with their "stickybob" seedheads to amuse those who have retained a schoolboy (or is that sexist?) sense of humour.* The road is fairly level to a junction with a lane on the right, where we turn left through a gate, joining the Offa's Dyke Path (ODP). Go up an enclosed track to a gate and climb to the next crest. This is a spur of Pentwyn and is also the highest point on the walk.

The path ahead is less definite, but still has a fence on the left and the remains of a wall on the right. Beyond a gate the path is more narrowly confined and soon arrives at a road. Turn left along the road, which descends quite steeply. *On coming round a bend the whole length of the Black Mountains can be seen stretching away beyond the Wye Valley. The ODP their crests—but that stretch is not covered in this book.* Pass the entrance to Pentwyn Farm on the left and cross over a stream. *Although this is not obvious, it marks the boundary from Herefordshire into Powys (Radnorshire)—from England into Wales.* Level with the next farm, Cae [Field]-Higgin, take a stile in the hedge on the right unless you want the quick return route to Rhydspence (in which case keep to the road for nearly 1¼ miles, keeping left at the only junction).

Bear left, as indicated by the waymark, down a field with clumps of gorse, aiming to the right of a large tree at the bottom, with a wide section of the Wye Valley ahead and to the left. *When reached the "tree" proves to be a hawthorn overtopped by an elder overtopped by an oak.* Take care to follow the ODP waymark at the bottom of the field as there are several other rights of way. Another stile or gate leads out onto a road on which you should turn right. *There are some fine wall pennyworts, with their waxy round leaves, on the wall on the right before a stream is crossed.* The road climbs past a house on the left to a track on the left at the top of a little rise.

The interior of Bettws Clyro Chapel

The chapel of ease of Holy Trinity, Bettws Clyro [Clear Water Chapel] is down this track. Although rebuilt since, it has connections with Francis Kilvert (see Introduction) and is a lovely simple little church with a 13th century font, 14th century roof and 15th century rood screen. On one occasion Kilvert conducted a christening here with ice floating in the font. At the time of writing the key can be borrowed from the bungalow (Aylton Lea) opposite the track. To reach the church go down the track and through a gate on the left, at which point the chapel can be seen across the field.

3. To continue the walk carry on along the road (or turn left after returning from the chapel). It is now narrow and climbs gently to a fork. Go left here. After about 500 yards ignore a gravel track which goes left to Upper Bettws. About 100 yards further on there are footpaths on either side. The one on the right is used on Walk 17, but we leave the ODP by turning left, over the stile. Head down to the gate in the far right corner. Go through two metal gates here and immediately turn left along the fence on the left. Keep to the fence or hedge on the left, pausing to admire the house and garden at Bettws Clyro, until there is a stile on the left.

Having climbed the stile head for a gate in the hedge ahead (somewhat to the left of the prominent Merbach Hill across the Wye). From this keep in the same direction across the next field to a stile about 70 yards from the corner on the left. Go over the stile into the next field and go down towards a prominent farm across the valley, to get to a gate from which the route is again down, with a hedge on the right.

Go down into the corner of the field, but instead of going out through the gate turn left to climb slightly, with a hedge on the right. Pass under a large oak tree and then a large beech (one of a clump of three). About 25 yards before the end of the field, and immediately after an ash tree, go over a stile down on the right. Turn left and climb with the fence and overgrown hedge on the left. Cross a stile in a wire fence coming up from the right and continue on the left of the field to the next hedge. Go through the gate and turn right, following the fence on the right down to the bottom corner of the field.

Go through (or, if necessary, over) the gate to the right beyond the derelict cottage (Old House) at the bottom of the field onto an enclosed lane to the left. This passes over a stream and bends right. Go through a gate and go along a ridge starting slightly to the right for the driest route through the next field. Pass a gate into the field on the left and a prominent clump of bramble on the right level with a clump of trees further into the field and then bear right to a waymarked stile about 40 yards from the top of the field. Go over this stile and cross a track to another one to continue in the same direction, heading slightly to the left of Merbach Hill (the nearest one with its wooded slopes going down steeply to the valley). You cross and then bear away to the left of the power lines, following a somewhat wandering sheep track. This should bring you to a metal gate from which there are good views of reaches of the Wye to the right and ahead.

Go through the gate and aim to the left of the conifer plantation which comes along from the right, still following the sheep track downwards. Aim for a prominent isolated tree and then for the corner of the field, in line with a grey house with a creeper on it. Leave the field through a gate and go to the left of the grey house to follow the road round to the starting point, crossing back into Herefordshire as you cross the stream.

16a
Rhydspence and Bettws Clyro

This is basically the second part of Walk 16 for those who did the shorter version.

Distance: *4¼ or 4½ miles.*

Start/by bus: *See Walk 16*

The Route

l. Start as though coming out of the front door of the Rhydspence Inn and turn left along the loop road. Pass the Powys sign, cross over the stream and then take a waymarked right turn over a stile or through the adjacent gate. Go through another gate, slightly to the left, going uphill in a narrow field with new houses to the left. As the field opens out head for a stile in the far right corner, still climbing. Beyond the stile keep to the right of the field, above trees which slope down to a stream in a little wooded valley (a *clough* in northern terminology). Two stiles lead into the next field, where the path is again on the

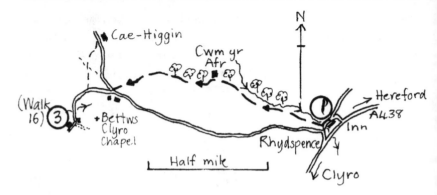

right. *The view behind is developing nicely, particularly along the Wye Valley to the south.*

Keep to the fence on the right after it bends right, with the gradient slacking off a little. Bend left with the fence towards the building of Cwm yr Afr, [Goat Valley] but keep outside the fence as it bends left as far as a stile on the right. Go over this and across the farm track to another stile. This leads into another field in which the route is again on the right above the clough. Cross the hedge at the top of the field by a stile and continue close to the fence on the right up to a waymark on a post. Turn left here to the leftmost of several gates in a hedge ahead. From the gate go across the next field to another gate slightly to the right, about halfway between the roofs (of Catworthy Court) and the corner of the field to the right.

This gate leads out into a road from which there are two ways to reach Walk 16 shortly before point 3. Anyone anxious to miss none of the Offa's Dyke Path (ODP) should turn right to Cae-Higgin and then take the path to the left. Anyone else should cross the first road to another, along which turn right.

Hay-on-Wye

Through the picturesque and historic village of Clyro, then a climb, mainly through farmland, onto Clyro Hill, with fine views of the Wye Valley. The return includes woods and the bank of the Wye.

Distance: *8 miles.*

Start: *By the clock tower at the junction of Broad Street and Lion Street in Hay-on-Wye, Grid ref. 229 424 (Landranger 198, Pathfinder 1016, Explorer 201). The main car park and the information centre are some distance away, at about 229 422. Car parking in Clyro (point 2 on the walk) is somewhat easier.*

By bus: *Buses passing through Hay-on-Wye between Brecon and Hereford are the 39 on weekdays (Stagecoach Red & White) and the 90 on Sundays (Yeomans Canyon Travel). In addition Roy Browns Coaches run the 445 service from Llandrindod Wells and Builth Wells on Wednesdays and Saturdays. All services also pass through Clyro.*

The English and Welsh (Y Gelli) names of the town both relate to a hedged enclosure in Norman times, although the town was first mentioned in a document of 944. It shows little sign of its past as a walled border stronghold. It has many buildings of the 18th and 19th centuries and a few from earlier. However even the 17th century mansion in the otherwise ruined Norman castle has been taken over by the almost ubiquitous second hand book trade. The fame of this means that there are plenty of places to stay and eat. A literary festival is held each year in May and June.

The Route

1. Start with your back to the clock tower of 1881 and the toilets, go ahead along Broad Street and turn left into Bridge Street. *(The Three Tuns, just beyond the turn, is originally 16th century.)* Bridge Street leads to the new Hay bridge (over the River Wye) which was opened in 1958 and strengthened in 1996. Cross the bridge and continue on the footway on the right, ignoring the waymark on the right for the Offa's Dyke Path, which will be the return route.

The road winds and climbs gently as far as a side road on the right. On the far side of this is the entrance to a caravan site. Go into this, through a facing gate and continue up beside the hedge on the left to a stile at the top of the field. Go over this.

The enclosure to the right contains an ancient Monk's Well, but nothing can be seen for nettles. Go diagonally across the next field in the direction of the waymark on the stile, losing height. *The village of Clyro (Clear Water) can be seen ahead, to the left at the bottom of a shallow valley, with a wooded hill to the left, and the much higher Clyro Hill some way to the right.*

Take the stile to the right of a gate and go across the next field in the direction of Clyro towards a stile on the left of a gate in the crossing hedge. *Tir-mynech (Monksland) Farm is to the right. A grange of the Cistercian Cwmhir Abbey was founded in Clyro in 1176, the gift of Clud of Elfael.*

Over the stile turn right alongside the hedge to a waymark which indicates the need to go diagonally left across the field to the far corner. Go over a stile on the right of two gates and keep the same direction through the next field to a gateway. *Clyro is now very clear ahead.*

Turn left before the gateway and in the next field descend with a fence on the right. Go over a stile in the corner of the field and go down the next field to the right hand end of a line of hawthorns. Here join a good path which goes ahead with a fence to the left.

The remains of Clyro Castle are on the hillock to the left. This was a Norman motte and bailey.

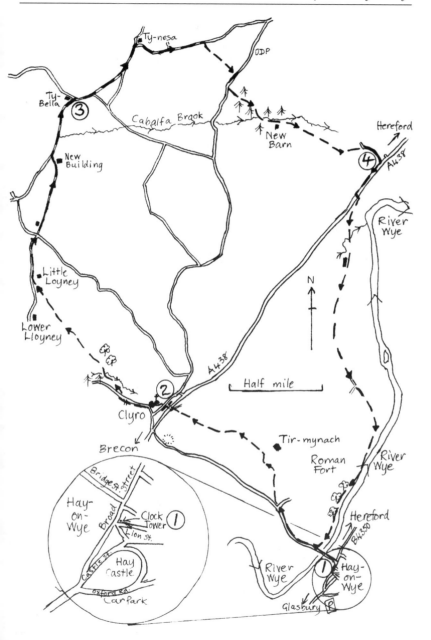

Ty-nesa

ODP

Ty-Bella

③

Cabalfa Brook

New Barn

Hereford

A438

New Building

River Wye

Little Loyney

N

Lower Lloyney

A438

Half mile

②

Clyro

Tir-mynach

Brecon

Roman Fort

River Wye

River Wye

Bridge St. Street

Hay-on-Wye

Broad St.

Clock Tower ①

Lion St.

Castle St.

Hay Castle

Oxford Rd.

Carpark

River Wye

Hereford

B4350

①

Hay-on-Wye

Glasbury

Unless you wish to explore the castle bear right from the fence corner, soon joining a better path which goes through a low-lying meadow. *There is an enclosure to the right, which probably contains a water plant—and I do not mean such as a bullrush!* Continue ahead when the clearest path goes left, to reach a stile. Go over this and turn left on a track which leads to the A438, which now avoids the centre of Clyro. Cross the road with care and go past the Kilvert Contemporary Art Gallery which has a fine Regency staircase window.

Soon you come to the old main road through the village of Clyro, with the Baskerville Arms Hotel (with an amusing signboard) to the right. *The name of the hotel refers to the local landlords. Their friend Sir Arthur Conan Doyle wrote the Sherlock Holmes tale of "The Hound of the Baskervilles", based on folklore concerning the Vaughan family of Hergest Court (near Kington) who were related to the Baskervilles. The story was set on Dartmoor to avoid upsetting the people of Clyro and Kington!*

The main claim to fame of the village of Clyro is that the Reverend Francis Kilvert (see Introduction), whose diaries give a fascinating view of life in the Welsh Borders in the 1870s, was a curate here from 1865 to 1872. The house in which he lodged is now the Art Gallery which you have just passed. Apart from the tower the church was rebuilt in 1853, and contains little of note.

2. Turn left, passing the Post Office, and then bear right into the churchyard through the lychgate, near which are some picturesque cottages and also a board giving interesting information about the village. Keep to the left of the church, passing up an avenue of yew trees, and fork right past the tower to leave the churchyard by a kissing gate. Turn right up the road, which has a footway on its left hand side. *On the right, beyond a rose-embellished whitewashed cottage, is the United Reformed Church and then there is a wooden cottage with eucalyptus trees in the front garden.* Just after the estate road of Begwyn's Bluff the footway ends.

Cross the other road to a signed footpath. Go over the stile and take the terraced path above the tennis court, dipping down into woodland, with Clyro Brook on the right. Go ahead through a gate and over a wooden bridge to continue between conifers, now with the brook on the left. Soon the path bears right and starts to climb. Go over or round a stile and up a steep climb. To leave the wood climb a stile on the left and turn right alongside the fence.

Behind is a fine view into the Wye Valley, with Hay Bluff being the prominent hill to the right of Hay and Lord Hereford's Knob, Rhos Dirion [Gentle Moor] and the isolated Mynydd Troed [Leg Mountain] successively further to the right. The gradient slackens off, increases and slackens off again. Keep above the slope down to the right to reach a wooden gate. Go through this and over the stile across a farm track. (The next four fields ahead are meadows with a fine variety of flowers in them.) Aim for a stile in the middle of the hawthorn and

Kilvert Contemporary Art Gallery, Clyro (was also Kilvert's lodging)

hazel hedge opposite, to the right of several gates. From this stile go ahead to a metal gate. *Lower Lloyney [Bushes] Farm is now over to the left and there is now a more extensive view behind.*

The path continues uphill aiming to the left of the farm ahead to a stile beside a metal gate and then in the next field to a stile to the left of the farm buildings and the tallest trees ahead, which are ash, poplar and hazel. Drop down to the road and turn right, soon passing Little Lloyney Farm which appears to be deserted but has a barn with vertical ventilation slits which look like those for firing arrows through from castles. When another road comes in from the right and the road bends left take the farm track ahead.

The track soon turns left into a farm, but the path continues ahead as an enclosed "green lane", which climbs steadily until it levels off, widens out and bears left to reach a track beside New Buildings Farm, where there is a collection of unusual poultry. Go through a gate and go ahead along the track to reach a road. Turn right along the road. On the left in about 600 yards, just before a junction, is a house, Ty Bella [Far House], with a fine collection of specimen trees in the garden.

Hay-on-Wye

3. Turn right here, with a sign to Clyro 2 miles. Keep left at the next fork, away from Clyro when a major road comes in from the right. Pass Penycae [Head of the field] Farm and turn right just before a cottage (Tynesa [Near House]) with a sign to Rhydspence. Continue along this road for about half a mile, passing a farm track to the left and a green lane and hardcore track into a field to the right.

Look out for a footpath sign on the right, which leads through a gate. Keep to the hedge on the left, going through a gap in a hedgerow into the next field to continue down. Go over a stile in the next crossing fence and cross the next field to a stile to the left of the large tree. Once over this turn right on the narrow tarmacked lane, joining the Offa's Dyke Path (ODP), which will take us back to Hay. *(The walk links with Walk 16 here.)* In a small dip an ODP acorn waymark indicates the way to the left down steps to a good path through a conifer plantation, with the Cabalfa [Place of the ferry (across the Wye)] Brook gurgling below to the right.

Just before a gate leading out of the wood take the rough track down to the right. After a spell beside the path the brook goes under a bridge which is not obvious. The path climbs again, up to the edge of the wood, near a decrepit barn in the field. *Ironically it is named New Barn!* From here the path turns left along the top of the wood for about 400 yards; it can be muddy underfoot and rather overgrown. *Although the bulk of the wood is coniferous, there is a variety of deciduous trees on the edge.* At a stile the path switches to be outside the wood until it descends left to a stile, which leads onto a tarmac track, which is followed down right to the A438.

4. Turn right along the road for about 500 yards, with good views of stretches of the Wye, keeping to the right hand verge (passing a layby in the process) until an ODP waymark indicates the way across the road (with care) to a stile. From this the path slants down to the right to pass through a copse. It then passes along the right hand side of a field, later switching to the left where there are trees on the bank of a stream heading for the river. The stream is crossed by a bridge with stiles either side and the waymark indicates the direction through the next field to a stile. From this the path heads for the left of farm buildings to a stile and gate.

On the other side of a farm track is a stile leading to a succession of fields where the immediate scenery is uninteresting, but that in the distance ahead is fine. The next field is a long one, but the path should be clear to a stile. Bear right from this stile to reach the hedge on the right and go along this, with it on the right. Before the end of the field turn right over an obvious stile which includes an odd carving entitled "OFFAR EX". Having climbed this turn left along a track which soon becomes enclosed, so that the only views are ahead. Cross another track and turn right to go along the right side of the next field, with a tall hedge on the right.

From the next stile bear right. The path reaches the river bank. In the next field, except in winter, the foliage on the riverside trees gives little chance of good views.

To the right is the site of a Roman fort but it is not very obvious. This may have been used as a temporary camp by Romans under Scapula in the 7th decade AD, and was turned into a Roman stronghold later, before being superseded by Brecon.

Go through a band of trees, coming out into a field in which you keep midway between the river and a wood on the right. The stile out of the field is near the river and the path then winds up into a stretch of woodland, and then contours higher above the river - but without improving the views. With the bridge over the Wye in sight ahead a stile leads to a flight of steps leading up to the B4361. Turn left to return over the bridge into Hay-on-Wye, with the castle in view above the town.

Mara Books

www.marabooks.co.uk

Mara Books publish a range of walking books for Cheshire and North Wales and have the following list to date. A complete list of current titles is available on our web site.

North Wales
Coastal Walks around Anglesey (volume 1)
ISBN 0 9522409 6 3. A collection of 15 walks which explore the varied scenery of Anglesey's beautiful coastline.

Coastal Walks around Anglesey Volume 2
ISBN 0 9522409 5 5. A companion volume to the above book, outlining 15 new walks spread around Anglesey's fascinating and beautiful coastline.

Circular Walks in the Conwy Valley
ISBN 0 9522409 7 1. A collection of 15 circular walks which explore the varied scenery of this beautiful valley from the Great Orme to Betws-y-Coed.

Walking on the Lleyn Peninsula
ISBN 1 902512 00 6. A collection of 16 circular walks which explore the wild and beautiful coastline and hills of the Lleyn Peninsula.

Walking in the Clwydian Hills
ISBN 0 9522409 3 9. A collection of 18 circular walks exploring the beautiful hills and valleys of the northern Welsh borders.

Walking in the Vale of Clwyd and Denbigh Moors
ISBN 1 90251208 1. A collection of 18 circular walks exploring the undiscovered country between the Clwydian Hills and the Conwy Valley.

Circular walks along the Offa's Dyke Path—Volume 1 Prestatyn to Welshpool
ISBN 1 902512 01 4. The first volume in a series of three which sample some of the finest sections of this well known national trail.

Walking in Snowdonia Volume 1—the northern valleys
ISBN 1 902512 06 5. 20 circular walks exploring the beautiful and dramatic valleys in the northern half of the Snowdonia National Park..

Cheshire
A Walker's Guide to the Wirral Shore Way
ISBN 1 902512 05 7. This book describes a linear walk of 23 miles following the old coastline between Chester and Hoylake.

Circular Walks along the Sandstone Trail
ISBN 0 9522409 2 0. The Sandstone Trail is Cheshire's best known and most popular walking route. This book gives a complete route description along with 12 circular walks covering the entire trail.

Circular Walks along the Gritstone Trail and Mow Cop Trail
ISBN 0 9522409 4 7. A route which follows Cheshire's eastern border along the edge of the Peak District. Following the same format as the Sandstone Trail book—a full description for both trails is combined with 12 circular walks.

Circular Walks in Wirral
ISBN 1 902512 02 2. A collection of 15 circular walks in the coast and countryside of Wirral.

Local History
Picturesque Wirral
ISBN 0 9522409 9 8. A reprint of part of T A Coward's "Picturesque Cheshire" dealing with Wirral, originally published in 1903. A fascinating glimpse of Wirral in the closing years of the nineteenth century.

Picturesque Cheshire—Chester and the Welsh border
ISBN 1 902512 03 0. Like the above, this is a reprint of two chapters from T A Coward's "Picturesque Cheshire", originally published in 1903, dealing with the city of Chester and the western limits of the county bordering Wales. A fascinating glimpse of this historic city in the closing years of the nineteenth century.